OTHER TITLES BY THE AUTHOR

Fire It Up: Building Restaurant Brands That Blaze
(2011 / Out of Print)

Stop Blasting My Mama: Make Email Marketing Work for Your Restaurant (2014 / Out of Print)

The Bullhearted Brand: Building Bullish Restaurant Brands That Charge Ahead of the Herd (2021)

Mass Behaving: Unlock the Power of Branding with Archetypes (2024)

Quiet Killers

What's Sabotaging Your Restaurant Brand's Growth & How to Stop It

Joseph Szala

Published by

BULLHEARTED PRESS

Quiet Killers
What's Sabotaging Your Restaurant Brand's Growth & How to Stop It
A Szalapalooza, LLC Publication

Published by Bullhearted Press
10420 Santa Fe Trail
Huntersville, NC 28078
(717) 968-4846
www.bullhearted.co

© 2025 Copyright by Joseph Szala and Szalapalooza, LLC. D/B/A Bullhearted
Printed in the United States of America.

First Edition January 2026

All rights reserved. No part of this book may be reproduced or transmitted in any form or by any means electronic or mechanical including photocopying, recording, or by an information storage or retrieval system, without the written permission of the publisher except where permitted by law.

ISBN 979-8-9940919-0-6

To my lovely wife, Elisa, my wonderful kids, Evelyn and Gabriel. You are my everything.

A note on AI Use

We live in an era where leaders, authors, journalists, and beyond are using AI more and more. I've noticed a steep uptick in raw AI generated writing being passed off as thought leadership. Therefore, I feel compelled to make clear how AI was used and not used in the writing of this book.

I used multiple AI engines to excavate research and help create correlative connections between my theories and the data that proves, or disproves them. The result was abandoning some of my initial thoughts as the data didn't actually support it. Bye bye Bias Loop!

AI was also used to quickly compile the bibliography because who really wants to do that? Not me. Sorry to my high school teacher who demanded we learn it.

Finally, when writing a book one reaches levels of writing fatigue. Things start to blend together and repetitive pacing and cadences can emerge. I am human, after all. In order to fix this, I used AI as a sort of editor to help me rethink what I wrote in order for the cadence to flow better and smoother. Hey, I'm anti-friction, right?

Here's where I did NOT use AI. I didn't use AI to write this book. The words are my own. The thoughts, my own. And yeah, I did actually use em-dash punctuation – everywhere you see it – because sometimes em-dashes are a powerful mechanism to drive home a point with added context. So, all those em-dashes were typed with my human fingers because my human brain told me it was the right use.

Contents

Forward 1

Intro 4

Part I: The Quiet Killers. 8

    Chapter 01: Quiet Killer 01: The Outdated Funnel 11

        The Funnel's Origins and Why It Never Fit Restaurant Behavior 11

        How Funnel Thinking Created Modern Customer Experience (CX) Debt. 16

        Google's Messy Middle and the Collapse of Linear Thinking 18

        When Funnel Logic Shows Up in the Real Restaurant World 21

        Why Digital Ordering Breaks the Funnel Completely 24

    Chapter 02: Quiet Killer 02: The Bias Loop 28

        Survivorship Bias: The Copycat Spiral That Breaks Restaurant Brands 28

        Confirmation Bias: The Part of Leadership Nobody Wants to Admit . . . 31

        When Survivorship Bias and Confirmation Bias Collide 33

        Case Study: Burger King Fights Dustiness with Mold. 36

Chapter 03: Quiet Killer 03: The Convenience Trap 40

    The Seductive Nature of "Easy"................................... 40

    How Shortcuts Become Systems 42

    The Technology Trap.. 45

    The Hard Way Pays: How Chipotle's Discipline
    Became Its Advantage... 47

    Case Study: Wendy's Dynamic Pricing Punch....................... 50

Chapter 04: Quiet Killer 04: Siloed Leadership & Fragmented Execution ... 53

    How Silos Formed in Restaurant Organizations And Why
    They Still Exist..53

    The Three Versions of the Brand 57

    What Fragmented Execution Looks Like and Why It's a
    System Problem, Not a People Problem 59

    Case Study: Red Lobster's Endless Shrimp Debacle 63

Part II: Setting the Record Straight.. 66

Chapter 05: How Guests Actually Behave 68

    The Death of the Linear Journey and the Rise of Real Human Behavior 68

    Why Guests Arrive With Intent, Not Curiosity 72

    Untangling Google's Messy Middle 74

    The Unique Volatility of the Restaurant Decision Loop................77

Chapter 06: Brand Clarity 80

    What Brand Clarity Actually Is And Why Most Brands Are Lacking It.. 80

    How Clarity Shapes Every Department's Decisions 83

Why Clarity Beats Creativity and Shortcuts 86

Clarity > Consistency > Trust > Behavior Change 89

Clarity Wins (and Clarity Misses) in the Real Restaurant World. 91

Case Study: First Watch's 2:30pm Power Move 93

Chapter 07: Alignment: Marketing, Tech, Finance & Operations
as One System. 96

Guests Ignore Your Org Chart. 96

Technology Is the Brand's Central Nervous System. 102

How Real Restaurant Brands Operationalize Unity. 104

Part III: The New Model 108

Chapter 08: Designing for Real Behavior 110

Experience Is the Brand, Not the Campaign 110

The Experience Chain: Exploration > Evaluation > Experience 113

Three Layers of One Behavioral Engine. 116

Designing Systems the Brain Loves 119

Key Takeaways: What Leaders Must Know Now 122

Action Items: What Leaders Must Do Now. 124

Chapter 09: Data-Backed Decision Making 127

People Lie, Data Doesn't. 127

How Data Exposes Friction 130

The Unified Data Model 134

Personalization, Prediction, and Platform Discipline 138

Case Study: Wing Stop Flies Higher with Data 140

Key Takeaways: What Leaders Must Know Now 142

Action Items: What Leaders Must Do Now. 144

Chapter 10: The Digital Front Door 148

Digital Is Now the First Door Guests Walk Through 148

The UX Patterns That Support Behavior 151

When Digital and Physical Must Match 154

Operational Truth Shapes Digital Design 157

Avoiding the Convenience Trap 158

Case Study: Cava Cracked Convenience. 162

Key Takeaways: What Leaders Must Know Now 164

Action Items: What Leaders Must Do Now. 167

Chapter 11: The Restaurant Brand Operating Model 172

The End of Departments and the Rise of Integrated Organizations . . .172

The Rhythms That Hold Integrated Organizations Together 175

Case Study: Due' Cucina and the Science of Consistency. 177

What Integrated Brands Actually Measure. 179

Integrated Organizations Don't Measure Effort. They Measure Reality 182

Scaling From 5 to 500: Why Integration Becomes a
Compounding Advantage. 185

Key Takeaways: What Leaders Must Know Now 189

Action Items: What Leaders Must Do Now............................191

Epilogue: The Future Belongs to Clarity 196

Field Guide: Tools for Leaders Who Refuse to Drift.......................... 200

    Quiet Killers Diagnostic...201

    The Clarity Operating System Map 203

    Monday Morning Audit 204

    The 90-Day Clarity Plan 205

Bibliography..210

Index 214

About the Author.. 222

Forward

I didn't plan to spend my life untangling restaurant systems. I thought tech was supposed to solve complexity, not multiply it.

But over the years, that's exactly where we've found ourselves: in the middle of half-built platforms, overlapping initiatives, and teams trying to move fast inside systems that were never designed to move together. Not always glamorous, but always real. And, somehow, always just a little messier than anyone wants to admit in the boardroom.

I started 3Owl in 2012. Back then, we did a little bit of everything. Over time, we zeroed in on multi-unit restaurants because that's where we saw the biggest opportunity — and the most frustration. For the last decade, we've worked with brands that are growing quickly, carrying legacy systems, trying to modernize, or all three at once.

We build digital infrastructure, which sounds clean and simple. In reality, it means living in the gap between strategy and execution. Between the menu and the POS. Between what the marketing team says and what actually shows up at the counter. That gap is where brands lose momentum. It's where guests get confused. And it's where we spend most of our time.

Joseph Szala, my business partner and our VP at 3Owl, has been in those rooms with me. We've walked into projects thinking the problem was design or tech, only to realize the real issue was structural. That the teams weren't aligned. That the system couldn't support the strategy. That the platform did what it was supposed to do but it wasn't the right platform in the first place.

For years, we saw the same issues repeating. We had different names for them. We tried to explain them in a dozen different ways. Then Joseph wrote this book and finally said it all clearly.

Quiet Killers names what so many people in this industry feel every day, whether they've found the words for it yet or not. It explains why a rebrand doesn't move the needle, even when the creative is great. Why the app you just launched isn't growing your loyalty adoption. Why your team is drowning in data but still unsure what's working.

We've seen it across nearly every client relationship we've had. A brand sets a bold growth strategy, invests in digital, launches a campaign but something stalls in the middle. The experience drifts. The execution feels scattered. The results are inconsistent, even though everyone involved is smart, committed, and doing their part.

Over the years, we've watched restaurant teams spend time and money solving the wrong problem. We've been guilty of that too. It's easy to think you need a better tech stack when what you actually need is shared clarity. Or that a loyalty campaign will drive frequency when the issue is operational trust. The patterns are repeatable. The drift is predictable. And the cost of not addressing it is real.

That's what this book offers: a way to see the system clearly. Joseph breaks down the invisible forces that slow down growth, not with more theory or abstract frameworks, but with behavioral truth, operational clarity, and the kind of cross-functional alignment that actually scales.

There's a line from Rory Sutherland I love: "The human mind does not run on logic any more than a horse runs on petrol." Restaurant guests don't run on logic either. They run on habit, instinct, coordination, and timing. When those things are out of sync, the brand suffers, no matter how smart the strategy is or how much data you have backing it.

This book won't make the work easier. But it will make it clearer. And clarity is what turns good teams into great ones.

Reading Quiet Killers reminded me of the first time I saw Moneyball. Not because it's about data, but because it challenges an entire industry to rethink what it values — and exposes the hidden forces that have been quietly working against progress for years.

Moneyball wasn't really about baseball. It was about questioning the rules everyone else accepted and building a system that actually reflects how things work. Quiet Killers does exactly that.

Once you start seeing the game differently, you never unsee it. And that's what makes this book so powerful.

Intro

Every restaurant brand has quiet killers. Hidden forces that undermine growth, create friction for guests, drain momentum from teams, and quietly corrode the experience long before anyone notices the symptoms. They don't show up on dashboards. They don't appear in brand guidelines. They rarely get named in meetings. Yet they determine whether a brand scales with confidence or collapses under its own complexity.

Brand leaders and agencies love complexity. They may not admit it, but in the meandering pages of 100-slide decks stuffed with clever charts that delight the eyes more than they illuminate the truth, complexity walks right in the front door. Sometimes it's insecurity disguised as intellectualism. Sometimes it's the belief that simplicity doesn't command the same price tag. Sometimes it's a boardroom culture that rewards "smart-sounding" over "useful."

Whatever the root, strategies balloon into overbuilt frameworks drenched in data meant to prove the plan is derisked. These decks satisfy boards, clients, and colleagues, but leave the people responsible for execution staring at beautifully packaged ambiguity. Teams splinter into their own interpretations. Everyone activates what they think the strategy says. No one is working toward the same reality because the strategy is unintelligible.

At the center of this all-too-common dynamic are four quiet killers operating just below the surface. Unnoticed or, worse, blindly trusted. Akin to the Biblical Four Horsemen of the Apocalypse, these killers undermine the team and company goals and rot away otherwise successful growth and futures. As with bullies and other types of enemies, if you don't face them and name them, you cannot eliminate them. With that in mind, it's time to haul them into the light, name them, and remove them from strategic thinking entirely.

The first quiet killer is blind faith in the Traditional Funnel. It simply does not reflect how people make decisions anymore. Modern behavioral research from Google, BCG, Archrival, and countless others shows guests do not travel neatly from awareness to consideration to purchase to loyalty. They loop chaotically through phases of exploration and evaluation, bouncing between social content, search, reviews, creators, habits, and past experiences. By the time a guest reaches your website, app, drive-thru, kiosk, or front door, they've already formed beliefs about your brand and decided what they want. A website visit is not a persuasion moment—it's a precision moment. And when brands design for persuasion instead of precision, they confuse guests, slow them down, and lose sales. Guest: frustrated. Brand: killed.

The second quiet killer is the Bias Loop: a destructive cocktail of Survivorship Bias and Confirmation Bias. Leaders study the industry, see what the biggest players (the survivors) are doing, and assume those behaviors created the success. Then they selectively gather evidence to confirm the imitation. This loop pushes emerging and mid-size brands toward strategies that don't match their stage, infrastructure, or reality. It's replication without context. Surface mimicry without the underlying foundation. A brand copies a tactic designed for a 1,500-unit powerhouse, tries to run it with a scrappy 10-unit system, and wonders why it collapses under its own weight.

Closely tied to this loop is the corrupted interpretation of "purpose." In the rush to mirror the Fortune 50 playbook, leaders now anchor their purpose to world-saving ideals instead of the real reason their brand exists. I love cheeseburgers as much as the next guy, but not once have I eaten one that was on track to cure climate change. Inflated, unfocused purpose statements pull leaders away from the core: real people, real problems, and authentic value.

These gaps create organizational drift, leading to the third quiet killer: Siloed Leadership and Fragmented Execution. Marketing chooses expressive creative over effective communication. Technology selects fast, convenient platforms without considering long-term flexibility. Operations optimizes processes that inadvertently contradict marketing promises. Training follows outdated standards. Analysts measure different success signals. Everyone is "doing their job," but no one is building the same brand.

Guests experience one brand through marketing, and an entirely different brand during the moments of truth—ordering, paying, waiting, and receiving. Internally, the brand is split across teams with different incentives, KPIs, data sources, and definitions of what success even means. When these groups don't operate as one system, the experience fractures in ways leaders often can't see. A thoughtfully designed app contradicts the in-store reality. Loyalty rewards slow throughput. Digital menus ignore kitchen capacity. Every break compounds until guests feel it—and quietly stop returning.

Finally there is the trap of convenience. No, not the convenience we seek to deliver to guests. It's opting for easy, convenient paths forward to avoid the difficult. Difficult decisions, processes, endeavors and even budgets and timelines create a visceral negative reaction. The excuses fly as to why something cannot or should not be done and soon enough the easier alternative is chosen. However, this kicks the can down the road and entraps teams to a handcuffed future. The easy choice today creates an even harder situation later because if you keep kicking that can down the road, eventually the road runs out and you're left with a pile of metaphoric cans.

Underneath these killers is a larger truth: Technology is no longer a department. It is the connective tissue of the modern restaurant. Ordering logic, menu architecture, pacing, pickup design, personalization, loyalty mechanics, and guest communication all rely on integrated systems that demand cross-functional leadership. Treating tech as a checkbox—to be assigned, not integrated—creates brittle systems that crumble under real-world pressure.

SpotlightAR's cross-functional research highlights this shift: industry-leading organizations now treat data, analytics, and technology as shared infrastructure, not isolated functions. Brands that treat tech as "another tool" fall into shortcut systems—fast to launch, impossible to scale, and fragile the moment real guests interact with them.

Quiet killers thrive when leaders use outdated models, make biased decisions, adopt technology without foundational thinking, and allow teams to operate independently. They remain invisible until they surface as slow drive-thru times, rising complaints, falling app conversions, inconsistent experiences across locations, frustrated guests, and slipping sales. Not because of one catastrophic error, but hundreds of small misalignments never tied to a single truth.

The cure is clarity. Clarity about how guests actually behave. Clarity about what the brand truly stands for. Clarity across teams. Clarity in the systems that run the experience. Clarity in the digital surfaces where most guests meet the brand for the first time. Clarity in how to design and operate a system that works in the real world.

This book will prove that clarity is not a soft concept. It is the most practical path to growth. We'll expose the quiet killers. Replace outdated assumptions with a real behavioral model. Rebuild the foundation with brand clarity and cross-functional alignment. Then design a modern experience system that works across web, app, kiosk, and physical operations.

If restaurant brands want to thrive in a nonlinear, high-expectation world, they must eliminate the quiet killers and build from clarity outward. This is the new way forward.

The Quiet Killers

Growth rarely ends with a catastrophic explosion. It ends with a gradual deceleration. It ends in the slow accumulation of friction that guests feel but leaders fail to see. It ends in the quiet acceptance of "good enough" operational standards. It ends in the safety of doing what the industry has always done.

We call these forces Quiet Killers for a reason. They do not announce themselves like a PR crisis or a failed health inspection. They hide in plain sight. They disguise themselves as standard operating procedures, best practices, and organizational heritage. They look like safety. They look like prudence. In reality, they are parasites feeding on the brand's momentum.

This section exposes the four most destructive mechanisms operating inside restaurant brands today. These are not theoretical risks. They are active threats destroying value in real-time.

The Outdated Funnel traps leaders in a linear fantasy of guest behavior that no longer exists. It forces marketing dollars into channels that guests ignore while neglecting the chaotic reality of how decisions actually happen.

The Bias Loop locks leadership into a cycle of imitation. It convinces emerging brands to copy the tactics of legacy giants without the infrastructure to support them. It mistakes survival for strategy.

The Convenience Trap seduces operators into choosing the easy path over the effective one. It prioritizes short-term relief for the internal team at the expense of long-term loyalty from the guest.

Siloed Leadership fractures the experience before the guest even walks through the door. It allows departments to optimize for their own metrics while the brand itself slowly disintegrates.

You cannot fix what you refuse to see. Most leaders prefer to look away because acknowledging these killers requires admitting that the comfortable way of doing business is over. It requires dismantling systems that took years to build. It requires confronting the ego that claims existing methods are sufficient.

Comfort is the enemy of growth. To build a brand capable of dominating the next decade, you must first purge the habits that defined the last one. We will drag these four killers into the light. We will examine exactly how they sabotage performance. We will strip away the corporate camouflage that keeps them hidden.

The takedown begins now.

CHAPTER 01

Quiet Killer 01: The Outdated Funnel

How a dead model quietly sabotages modern restaurant brands.

The Funnel's Origins and Why It Never Fit Restaurant Behavior

To understand why restaurant brands stumble into the same pits year after year, look at the diagram that refuses to die. The funnel served as more than a framework. It became a worldview. It offered generations of marketers a hallucination of order along with a sense that customer behavior was predictable if you simply lined up the right messages in the right sequence. It made messy

Quiet Killer 01: The Outdated Funnel

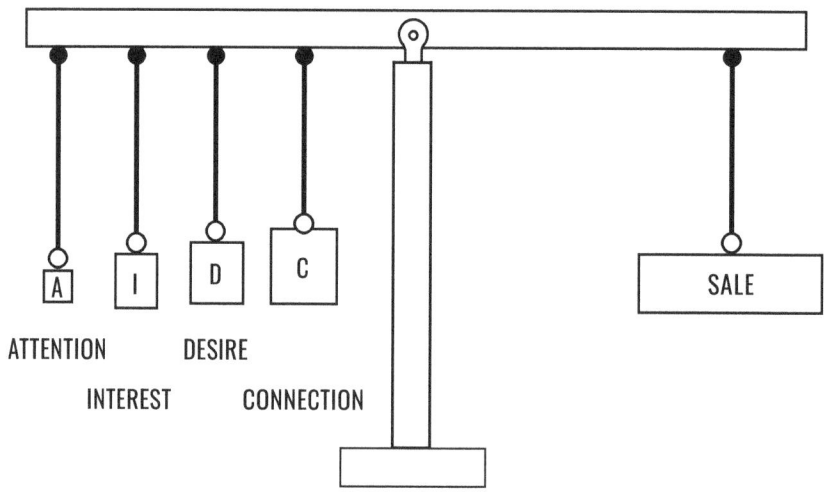

fig A. – E. St. Elmo Lewis' AIDA Model Diagram, circa 1858

human impulses feel manageable. Leaders believed they could persuade people into behaving the way the brand preferred. That fantasy has survived for more than a century. The restaurant industry inherited it without ever stopping to ask whether it matched reality.

The truth is harsh in its simplicity. The funnel fails restaurants because the architects never designed it for them. They ignored categories with fast decisions, high frequency purchases, or situational triggers like hunger and convenience. The funnel belongs to a pre-digital world where marketers genuinely believed they could engineer desire by pushing people along a carefully crafted sequence. First you make them aware. Then you make them consider. Then you get them to buy. Loyalty supposedly develops sometime after. This linear progression is completely wrong in today's reality.

You need to look at the origin to see the misalignment. Around 1898, an advertising pioneer named E. St. Elmo Lewis attempted to codify how people might move from attention to action. He observed what he believed were stages of persuasion and turned them into the AIDA model. (See fig. A) That stands for Attention, Interest, Desire, Action. Originally, this was a scale rather than a funnel. Sales teams used it rather than marketing teams. The goal was to tip the scale into a sale by stacking attention, interest, and desire. In theory, you add the right ingredients and you get the sale.

This was groundbreaking at the time because the consumer environment was small. Choices were limited. Products were novel. Purchasing often required deliberate thought. Marketers had the luxury of assuming customers were listening because customers often were. Newspapers, early radio, and in-store salespeople formed the backbone of persuasion. The funnel worked well enough for industries with long consideration cycles like appliances, insurance, banking, and cars.

Restaurants operate in a different psychological landscape. Back then, restaurants were a luxury or a roadside fix featuring a short order cook and cheap coffee. Today, guests decide where to eat based on impulses, cravings, routines, habits, and constraints. They do not enter a formal awareness stage. They live their lives, encounter cues, and act. They choose what is close or familiar or fast. They eat emotionally and reactively. No linear progression exists.

Yet brand marketers adopted the funnel wholesale. Agencies imported it into their pitch decks. Executives found comfort in its simplicity. Nobody questioned it because it looked strategic. It created a sense of progression. It turned chaos into order. Even today, you will hear leaders talk about top-of-funnel impressions and lower-funnel conversion tactics without acknowledging that the average guest chooses a place to eat in under two minutes. This happens after dozens of subconscious micro-influences that the brand neither controls nor fully understands.

This creates a massive problem. Models that are elegant but inaccurate are dangerous.

The funnel assumes persuasion. It assumes nurturing. It assumes people need to be led by the hand through a rational journey toward choosing your brand. But restaurant guests rarely behave rationally. Behavioral economists have proved that people make decisions based on shortcuts, heuristics, emotion, and environmental cues. Google's research on decoding decisions crystallized this reality. Customers do not move through a series of steps. They bounce through two mental modes called exploration and evaluation. They do this repeatedly until something triggers enough confidence to take action. They oscillate and meander while collecting informational artifacts for or against your brand.

Restaurants operated in a category defined by immediacy long before Google ever mapped that behavior. Even in the early 2000s, people chose restaurants based on proximity and cravings. The funnel failed to explain that behavior. It actively misunderstood it.

The model stuck because restaurant organizations needed a way to compartmentalize responsibility as they scaled. Marketers needed assurances and a de-risked approach that got buy-in from colleagues. The funnel created clean swim lanes. Brand teams owned awareness. Digital teams owned consideration. Operations owned conversion. Loyalty teams owned retention. Everyone felt they had a place in a larger system. The funnel made internal alignment feel logical even as guest experiences became more fragmented. The funnel became gospel because it served as a mainstay in every university marketing course.

This is where the real damage happened. Brands designed for the funnel rather than the guest.

Brands of all sizes were forced into funnel-led strategies despite availability of resources. Marketing efforts focused on awareness. Position the brand. Spray and pray with television, radio, billboards, and direct mail. Conversion was ignored as a problem for the next stage in the funnel journey. These efforts became top targets for board rooms as they evaluated investments against returns. Funnel marketing became a fool's errand and a recipe for wasted dollars for startup brands that lacked the funds to activate a full funnel strategy.

Look at how websites evolved. Early restaurant sites were simple menus with hours and locations. The funnel mindset burrowed deeper and homepages became cluttered with campaigns, banners, lifestyle imagery, and multi-step flows. Designers created paths to match theoretical stages. Brands asked how to move guests from interest to consideration instead of asking what the guest wanted to do right now. The answer was almost always more content and more persuasion. The guest just wanted to order lunch but was forced to wade through a funnel-flavored swamp.

The same thing happened to apps. Nearly every restaurant app opened with a splash screen, an onboarding flow, or a loyalty signup before allowing someone to place an order. This is pure funnel logic. Capture them early. Nurture them often. Push them deeper into your world. Apps are tools rather than brochures. Tools should not get in the way of the mission. Brands operating under the gravity of the funnel missed that distinction.

Even the rise of digital ordering failed to dislodge the model. Brands layered funnel concepts on top of high-intent behaviors. They created unnecessary steps, promotional interruptions, and brand moments inserted into flows where they do not belong. The mindset continued to prioritize building awareness and consideration. These goals are catastrophically wrong in this context. The moment a guest opens your digital front door is an invitation to get out of their way. You must deliver a convenient path to order.

Trace the lineage of most modern restaurant UX problems and the origin point is always the same. Someone believed the guest needed persuading at a moment when the guest actually just needed to eat. A model created in the nineteenth century still manages to undermine twenty-first century restaurant experiences. It is persistent because teams rarely question it.

The funnel deserves to be questioned. It deserves to be dismantled. It deserves to be buried so deeply that it never again distorts the way you design for behavior you can measure. Remove the funnel from the decision-making process and you expose the flaws in the system. Guests stop fighting your interfaces. Teams stop arguing over irrelevant stages. Technology stops being forced into unnatural shapes. Operations stop feeling the downstream burden of broken flows.

The wreckage of the funnel is everywhere you look. It is time to stop building on top of it.

How Funnel Thinking Created Modern Customer Experience (CX) Debt

Funnel thinking trained restaurant brands to persuade in the wrong moments. It conditioned teams to believe the guest needed convincing at the exact moment they were already ready to act. It pushed design teams to turn the homepage into a carnival of campaigns and encouraged product teams to put loyalty sign-ins before the menu. Leaders interrupted ordering flows with modal windows screaming about points and perks because the funnel treated the guest like a lead in a pipeline. The guest showed up hungry.

That mismatch birthed modern CX debt.

Funnel logic made brands believe the digital journey was a sequence of steps to control. Funnels insist that people move predictably. Guests move with urgency and divided attention. They move with low blood sugar while driving into a parking lot. Funnels force linear progression while behavior is chaotic. This creates a conflict between the interface and the brain. Daniel Kahneman distinguishes between System One thinking, which is fast and intuitive, and System Two, which is slow and analytical. Funnels force guests into System Two by demanding they process marketing copy and navigation hurdles. Guests want to stay in System One. They want to use mental shortcuts to get food fast.

When a brand treats the digital journey like a sales pitch the entire experience becomes a maze. The homepage morphs into a billboard that demands interpretation. The menu starts behaving like a content hub rather than a functional tool. The loyalty program stops being an incentive and becomes a negotiation. The system treats the guest like a captive audience even though the guest came to eat.

This is the debt. Debt always compounds.

You see funnel logic in the places where friction appears first. Video-heavy homepages built to be cinematic rather than functional. Hero images stacked above the menu that force guests to scroll before they can see food. Loyalty prompts blocking access until account creation is complete. None of these decisions come from operations. They come from persuasion logic built for ecommerce.

Data exposes the cost of this logic. The Baymard Institute found that forced account creation increases abandonment by up to 82 percent. Restaurant behavior follows the same pattern because hunger tightens the clock. Guests are trying to complete the job rather than evaluate the brand. Google's mobile benchmarks show that a one-second delay in load time can reduce conversion by 20 percent. Yet many restaurant homepages take five to seven seconds to load because they are bloated with creative assets built for brand vanity. These decisions come from the funnel.

This is the heart of CX debt. Design teams optimize for persuasion while guests optimize for speed.

Those two intentions collide at the moment of ordering. Every collision creates friction. Friction increases cognitive load. The human brain fights hard to avoid cognitive load because it requires effortful processing. When a brand forces a guest to think about navigation or close a pop-up window, they increase the cognitive burden. A brand aligned with a clear archetype and simple behavior reduces this load and builds trust. High cognitive load kills conversion.

Restaurant behavior tells a different story. Guests arrive in a state of intention. They are already halfway through the decision process before the brand ever sees them. Neuroscience research by Antonio Damasio proves that emotion drives decision making long before logic enters the picture. The decision to eat is an emotional marker that precedes the rational act of ordering. Guests do not need persuasion inside the flow because the emotional decision has already been made. They need direction.

Funnel thinking reverses the sequence. It inserts persuasion into the wrong moment. It assumes the guest is undecided when the guest is impatient. It assumes the guest needs to be convinced when the guest needs to be carried.

This disconnect creates a pileup of unnecessary screens and messages. A team of cognitive scientists at University College London found that people subconsciously abandon tasks when cognitive strain spikes. Restaurants call this mystery abandonment. It is actually misaligned intention.

The industry has treated the funnel like gospel because funnels make sense to internal teams. They create order and predictability. They give marketers a narrative and product teams a map. But funnels reflect how organizations wish behavior worked rather than how it actually works. The guest journey never was a funnel.

Funnel thinking created CX debt because it forced the brand to solve the wrong problem. Brands solved for persuasion and hierarchy instead of hunger and speed. They built systems that made sense on a whiteboard yet collapsed under real human behavior. Digital systems must match the operating reality of the kitchen and the psychological reality of the guest. Debt becomes inevitable when they do not match. That debt becomes expensive the longer it lives inside the system.

Google's Messy Middle and the Collapse of Linear Thinking

Clarity emerges only when a brand accepts the reality of human decision making. Nothing has exposed that reality more clearly than Google's Messy Middle research. The Messy Middle serves as the behavioral map that replaced the funnel. It shows how guests loop, compare, abandon, return, stall, accelerate, and switch without any linear pattern. It reveals the chaos funnels tried to hide.

The funnel offers a comforting fiction while the Messy Middle presents the uncomfortable truth. It destroys the logic that held marketing strategy together for decades. Google uncovered a chaotic loop involving an endless back and forth between exploration and evaluation rather than a neat sequence. Shortcuts,

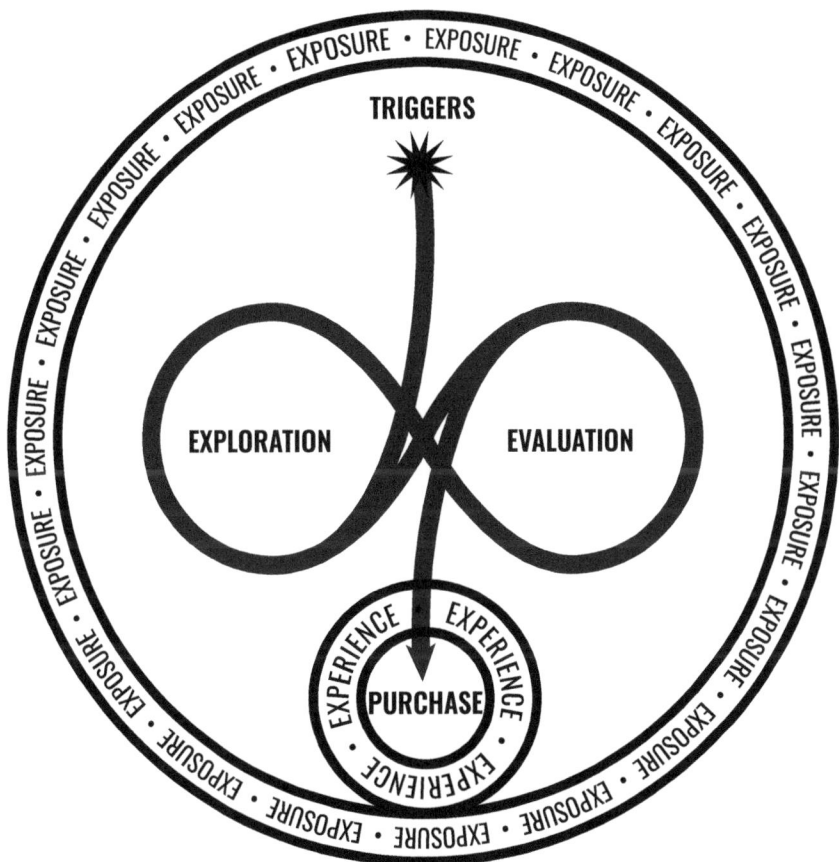

fig B. – Google's Messy Middle Diagram, circa 2020 (redesigned)

habits, heuristics, and confidence building signals power this loop instead of persuasion.

Restaurant operators have always known this. They watch guests switch constantly between options. They see people step out of line after waiting too long. They watch guests scroll through Yelp while standing in front of the menu board. They see loyalty members abandon points collection because the process requires too much effort. The restaurant industry lived inside the Messy Middle long before anyone gave it a name.

Google put structure around the chaos by identifying two distinct mental modes. Exploration involves expanding and surfacing possibilities. Evaluation involves narrowing and deciding among them. Customers bounce back and forth between these modes rather than proceeding neatly from one to the other. They zoom out to explore. They zoom in to evaluate. They get interrupted and restart. This loop happens for hours when booking a vacation or for thirty seconds when choosing lunch.

This loop matters for restaurants because it reveals a critical flaw in funnel logic. People do not get persuaded into action. They get buy-in through confidence.

Confidence comes from clarity and consistency. It comes from authenticity and predictability. It comes from trust and ease.

A beautifully shot campaign fails to create confidence. Highly styled photography often serves as an inauthentic cue rather than a signal of quality. People see perfectly styled images of food as lies. They know their burger will look different in real life. Real imagery found on social channels gets more traction because it builds belief.

Research from BCG adds another layer to this dynamic. Modern consumers live in a constant cloud of micro influences like search results, map listings, friends' posts, creator recommendations, pickup ETA times, convenience heuristics, and habitual stops. These influences happen outside of the brand's control yet determine whether someone moves from exploration into action. The decisive moments happen before the brand ever gets the chance to funnel someone toward a decision.

The funnel collapses under modern behavior because it assumes a captive path.

The Messy Middle proves the guest is in complete control. The funnel assumes the brand orchestrates the journey. The Messy Middle shows confidence is the engine. The funnel tells you to decorate the top of your digital surfaces. The Messy Middle tells you to optimize the moment of action.

Restaurants win by clearing the path people are already walking rather than pushing them forward.

Funnel thinking breaks dramatically here because it encourages brands to design for the wrong moment. Assuming guests arrive early in the journey leads brands to greet them with videos, campaigns, promos, category education, and brand narrative. The Messy Middle tells us guests arrive having already explored and evaluated. That top of funnel content becomes a noisy interruption at the worst possible time.

Restaurant brand leaders often miss this contradiction because the funnel has played in the background of their careers for years. Seeing the Messy Middle clearly changes everything. You stop imagining guests moving through a content ladder. You stop obsessing over awareness driving creative. You start accepting that your digital front door acts as the endpoint of a process you did not design and cannot control.

The Messy Middle forces a more honest question. What does the guest need to feel confident taking the next action? Answering that question sharpens the entire experience. Ignoring it dulls everything.

The Messy Middle is the operating reality for every restaurant brand competing for attention in a world where thousands of tiny influences shape every meal decision. It demands that brands abandon the fantasy of choreography and embrace the truth of facilitation. It demands that brands become easier, faster, clearer, and more predictable. It demands that funnel thinking give way to behavioral thinking.

When Funnel Logic Shows Up in the Real Restaurant World

Funnel logic clutters interfaces while altering organizational behavior. It shapes decisions that feel harmless in isolation yet prove destructive in practice. Treating the guest journey like a sequence of persuasion steps causes every department to optimize for its own version of success. Marketing chases visibility while Digital chases engagement. Loyalty chases sign-ups while Technology chases stability. Operations chases throughput. Each team believes it works in service of the guest. The outcomes rarely line up that way.

This misalignment shows up as drift inside most brands. The experience pulls in different directions. The menus get busier. The homepage becomes heavier. The ordering flow becomes more layered. Loyalty prompts appear earlier. Campaigns appear in places no guest expects. Funnel thinking causes this because it rewards steps and screens instead of movement. It views the journey through dashboards rather than human behavior. Taking that mindset converts everything into a performance for internal metrics instead of a pathway for real people in real moments.

Guests feel this friction long before anyone inside the organization notices. It manifests as hesitation. A pause before tapping. A moment of recalibration. A second of doubt. Hunger ignores doubt while time pressure magnifies it. Behavior shifts quietly here. Guests do not complain. They do not warn the brand. They do not articulate disappointment. They simply adjust their path. They take the easier channel. They avoid the step that added work. They drop off when the flow demands too much attention.

Small shifts eventually become patterns. They appear in digital analytics as lower conversion during peak hours. They appear in operational reports as spikes in walk-ins when digital friction grows. They appear in loyalty dashboards as stalled engagement. They appear in search data as guests exploring alternatives. The patterns spread slowly. They create symptoms that look like performance problems instead of behavioral responses. Leaders chase the wrong solution because the system hides its own impact.

Funnel logic exacts a heavy cost here. It produces a journey that works against itself. It introduces tension between departments that were meant to function as one system. It embeds friction into decisions that were supposed to create clarity. It leads to adoption of technologies that solve internal desires while complicating external realities. It amplifies the gap between what the brand thinks it delivers and what the guest actually experiences.

Behavioral science has proved for decades that the human brain abandons tasks when cognitive effort rises past an invisible threshold. Researchers at University College London found that even mild increases in cognitive load trigger avoidance behaviors especially when the goal is simple. Restaurant ordering sits firmly in that category. The task is basic. The expectation is speed. The tolerance is low. The instinctive reaction to confusion is exit rather than irritation. The guest moves on because the brain prefers certainty even when the alternative comes from another brand.

Funnel thinking fails to handle this reality because it imagines a shopper with time and patience. Restaurant guests behave more like commuters trying to beat a light. They are completing a need rather than choosing a product. They want a system that moves with them rather than a system that demands interpretation.

The tension grows as the brand adds more channels. Walk-in, Digital, Pickup, Drive-thru, and Delivery all become opportunities for drift. Funnel logic tries to control these touchpoints through messaging and promotion. It attempts to manufacture a journey rather than listen to the one that already exists. The kitchen absorbs the consequences. The staff absorbs the uncertainty. The guest absorbs the friction.

The Messy Middle changes that understanding entirely. It shows the true pattern of human movement. The guest loops and scans. They return. They pause and resume. They follow instinct rather than instruction. They respond to clarity rather than content. They complete the journey when the path feels obvious rather than when the brand persuades them. This applies to every part of the restaurant experience. The drive-thru lane and the pickup shelf play by the same rules as the dine-in flow and the handoff moment. Every step reinforces confidence or interrupts it.

Funnel logic ignored hunger, pressure, context, and pace. It assumed a rational customer who welcomes more information. Modern restaurant behavior contradicts that assumption in every direction. Guests want the fastest path to certainty. They want predictable timing. They want clean instructions. They want the brand to tell them what to do and get out of the way. This is functional rather than emotional.

Restaurant brands that adapt to this truth build experiences that reduce cognitive work. They reorganize the journey around momentum instead of persuasion.

They use data to identify friction long before the guest disengages. They align marketing, operations, and digital around one shared objective to make the path effortless.

The Messy Middle supports this shift as a behavioral model. It protects brands from building journeys based on outdated assumptions. It forces organizations to design for movement rather than message. It gives teams a shared truth that the guest chooses the simplest option that meets their intention. Loyalty forms naturally if the brand becomes that option. The guest follows the path of least resistance somewhere else if the brand fails.

Real work begins here. Understand the movement. Design the system. Eliminate the drift. Rebuild the journey around the principle the funnel never understood. Clarity drives behavior.

Why Digital Ordering Breaks the Funnel Completely

Digital ordering is the reality check the funnel never survived. It exposes the model's flaws with brutal clarity. When someone opens an app or a website to order food, they are not entering a staged journey. They are entering a task. Tasks reject theatrics.

Digital ordering is intent distilled. It is the moment of action. The only thing a guest wants at that moment is speed, simplicity, and accuracy. Every time a brand forces messaging into that moment—storytelling, promotions, value props, loyalty pushes, secondary calls to action—it violates the guest's intention. The funnel demands that the brand interrupt the user to create value. The user defines value as the absence of interruption.

To understand the severity of this disconnect, look at the bifurcation of experience in the modern restaurant landscape.

Consider your standard restaurant brand experience that operates under funnel logic. The guest goes to the brand's website because they are hungry. The first thing they see is a splash screen inviting them to join a loyalty program. They close it. The homepage loads a carousel of hero images promoting three different limited-time offers. The guest ignores them and hunts for the menu button. Once they hit that button, they're asked if they want pickup or delivery. The selection pushes them over to a completely different website experience on an ordering platform site. Oftentimes, they have to start the process over in selecting delivery or pickup, then the associated address. But fine, they go through it because they're hungry. Once in the menu, they select a burger. A modal window pops up asking if they want to make it a meal. They decline. They go to checkout. Another prompt appears asking them to sign up for email updates to receive five dollars off their next order. Then they get hit with upsell offers. They tap through a multi-step checkout process while re-entering information or struggling to log in. They get through it and, finally, they pay.

This experience treats the guest as a captive audience member who needs to be educated and upsold. The brand views every screen as a billboard. The guest views every screen as a barrier. The funnel dictates that awareness and consideration must be reinforced at every step. The guest experiences this as friction. The brand believes it is optimizing revenue. The guest believes the brand is wasting their time.

Now consider a brand experience with a better path. This brand operates under behavioral logic. The guest opens the website. The interface recognizes that it is 6:00 PM and the guest is at home. The homepage displays a "Reorder Last Meal" button front and center. The menu is a simple list without large lifestyle photography pushing content below the fold. The guest taps the item. They tap checkout. Apple Pay activates immediately. The order is placed in fifteen seconds.

This brand understands that the guest did not come to the app to learn about the brand. They came to eat. The brand removed the funnel entirely. They replaced persuasion with utility. And throughout the process, the brand's tone of voice and visual identity is clear and powerful without impeding on the task at hand.

This distinction explains why the best digital ordering experiences feel almost invisible. They avoid shoving the brand's story in the way of ordering. They avoid performing. They avoid guiding the guest emotionally. They let the guest finish the job quickly and intuitively. Intuitive systems that make tasks easy earn trust. Trust is earned because the brand removed barriers rather than exploiting the moment to force marketing and messaging.

Restaurants that thrive digitally understood this early. They stripped away unnecessary screens. They reduced cognitive load. They simplified menu categories. They clarified calls to action. They eliminated detours. Their funnels were discarded.

Yet the funnel still lives in the digital pathways for many brands. It tells designers to decorate instead of simplify. It tells marketers to promote instead of clarify. It tells operators to adjust for digital flaws instead of fix them.

Digital ordering punishes this mindset. Guests abandon when the process becomes cumbersome. They bounce when the path is unclear. They get annoyed when the app tries to engage instead of execute. They go elsewhere when the ordering experience feels like work. This frustration happens in seconds rather than minutes.

The cost of this friction is higher than a lost sale. It is a lost habit. Digital ordering is built on habit formation. Habits are formed through repetition and reward. In the context of food ordering, the reward is not just the food. The reward is the ease of acquisition. When a brand inserts funnel-based friction into the process, they punish the user for attempting to form a habit. The brain categorizes the app or website as difficult or annoying. The next time hunger strikes, the brain will suggest a path of less resistance which is usually a third party platform like Doordash or Ubereats.

Leaders often fail to connect these outcomes back to the funnel. They look at KPIs and blame low conversion or weak loyalty strategy or creative not resonating. They rarely blame the root cause, which is a linear persuasion model pasted onto a nonlinear behavioral reality.

The funnel fails because it misdiagnoses the moment. Digital ordering succeeds when the brand honors the moment.

Once a brand understands this, the entire foundation of their digital experience changes. You stop building for awareness. You stop designing for persuasion. You stop believing you can nurture someone into ordering a burger they already decided to buy. You begin designing for clarity, intent, and speed. These are the actual engines of restaurant decision making.

When the funnel collapses, clarity emerges. Clarity is the only thing strong enough to carry a modern restaurant brand forward. That is why this book starts here. Not with creativity. Not with technology. Not with operations. But with a funeral.

The funnel is dead.

The moment you stop trying to revive it, your brand can finally start to live in the world your guest already occupies.

CHAPTER 02

Quiet Killer 02: The Bias Loop

How common biases fool leaders into believing doomed strategies

Survivorship Bias: The Copycat Spiral That Breaks Restaurant Brands

Restaurant leaders rarely believe they are making biased decisions. Bias is something other people fall victim to. In our own minds, we're rational, seasoned, and observant. We're the people who've "seen enough" to know what works. But that sense of certainty is exactly what makes survivorship bias so dangerous. It tricks smart leaders into drawing conclusions from incomplete information. It convinces people that the visible successes are the whole story and that copying those successes is the safest path forward. In restaurants, this bias is everywhere, shaping decisions about technology, brand positioning, digital experience, menu structure, loyalty, promotions, and even interior design.

Survivorship bias begins with an illusion: that the brands at the top did everything right, and that what they're doing now is what made them successful. The truth is far messier. Enterprise restaurant brands are the survivors not because every tactic they use is brilliant, but because time, scale, real estate leverage, brand memory, and enormous operational infrastructure keep them standing even when they make mediocre decisions. A global burger brand can survive a dozen bad app updates. A 20-unit fast casual cannot. One plays on legacy. The other plays on precision.

But survivorship bias makes smaller brands emulate the wrong things. They mimic the visible tactics of giants—their rewards programs, their TikTok content, their menu layout, their kiosks, their brand campaigns—without understanding the invisible systems underneath. Enterprise brands can absorb complexity because they have training pipelines, staffing levels, engineering resources, years of A/B testing, data science teams, and frameworks for rolling out changes across thousands of stores. Smaller and emerging brands do not.

Another reality of the top brands that is often overlooked is the reality of the era in which they were founded. Even 7 years ago was a much different world than today. People's behaviors have shifted. Technology has advanced. Expectations have evolved. Therefore, the foundations of how a brand starts then, is wildly different than today.

Yet the logic persists: "McDonald's does it, so it must work."

Except McDonald's can make almost anything work because their system protects them from themselves. It's a brand with nearly 100 years of nostalgia, trial and error, learnings, and evolution baked into today. A brand with 12 locations doesn't have that luxury.

Survivorship bias is why so many restaurant brands end up with digital experiences that feel bloated, inconsistent, or painfully generic. They replicate loyalty mechanics they saw in a national chain without realizing those mechanics only work when you have millions of monthly active users and an entire CRM team working behind the scenes. They redesign their interior flow to match a category leader without noticing the footprint difference, or the labor model difference, or the staffing reality of Tuesday nights when no one is around to police the ordering line.

Survivorship bias convinces teams the survivors succeeded because of their visible features. It hides the failures. It hides the brands that tried the same tactic and collapsed. It hides the internal scaffolding that made success possible. It hides the operational discipline that keeps everything consistent. It hides the sunk cost of previous failures. And it hides the fact that many enterprise decisions aren't good. They're just survivable.

When you look at the top 50 U.S. restaurant chains, you're not looking at "best practices." You're looking at the winners of a decades-long endurance race. Many of them succeeded because of brand memory, early market entry, footprint strategy, prime real estate, franchising networks, or sheer ubiquity. Their current tactics, the things smaller brands eagerly copy, are often the least responsible for their success.

Yet the industry copies them anyway.

Survivorship bias is why emerging brands choose platforms far too complex for their needs. It's why they build loyalty programs too intricate for their base. It's why they over-design digital flows. It's why they prioritize flashy features over foundational clarity. They're mimicking giants assuming the giant got there by doing those things. The reality is the giant succeeded for reasons that often have nothing to do with the APIs, menu hero images, or fridge-to-app personalization features that get copied downstream.

This bias becomes even more damaging because it feels reasonable. It feels logical to emulate winners. It feels smart to adopt what's proven. Leaders often believe they're minimizing risk by copying enterprises, when in fact they're replicating decisions that only work at enterprise scale, or only work because the brand can afford for them not to work.

The irony is painful: the more a small or mid-sized brand copies a giant, the more it unintentionally sabotages itself. Because the very things a giant can survive will sink a brand without the infrastructure to absorb friction.

Quiet Killers   31

Survivorship bias is the first half of the Bias Loop.

The second half is even more dangerous because it reinforces the first. This is where belief becomes blindness.

Confirmation Bias: The Part of Leadership Nobody Wants to Admit

If survivorship bias provides the spark, confirmation bias supplies the oxygen. This activates the bias loop at full force. Once a team convinces itself that a certain strategy or platform is the right move, confirmation bias kicks in to turn that assumption into a self-reinforcing truth. It transforms a hypothesis into a mandate before anyone has validated the premise.

Confirmation bias works subtly. It hides under phrases claiming that the data supports a decision or that the guest expects a certain feature. Leaders use these phrases even when those statements lack meaningful testing. Leaders selectively interpret data by prioritizing anything that supports their preferred direction while dismissing anything that does not. They treat supportive metrics as gospel. They treat contradictory metrics as noise. This explains why brands repeat failed tactics. It explains why they choose platforms that fail to fit. It explains why they double down on decisions that introduce friction.

This bias frequently appears in tech adoption within restaurants. A vendor demo shows a slick AI ordering feature. The enterprise chain down the street announces a pilot of the same thing. Thought leadership articles declare AI as the future. The fear of missing out overrides the need for utility. Internal conversations shift immediately. They stop asking if the brand should do this. They start asking how fast they can implement it. The momentum operates on emotion rather than reason. Confirmation bias goes looking for evidence to justify the emotional commitment once it is made.

The team filters out warnings. Usability tests showing confusion get dismissed as edge cases. Operations pushback about throughput gets dismissed as a training issue. Guest complaints about friction get judged as resistance to change. The leadership team convinces themselves that the friction is temporary. They believe the guest just needs to learn the new behavior. They ignore the reality that guests refuse to learn behaviors that make their lives harder.

This behavior extends beyond restaurants into human nature. Leaders often prefer being right over becoming right. They prefer reinforcing their assumptions to challenging them. That tendency becomes particularly strong in fast-paced environments where leadership is overwhelmed and timelines are compressed. Executives feel pressure to have answers. Confidence often masquerades as clarity in those conditions. A decisive leader feels safer than an inquisitive one.

Confirmation bias also appears in branding. A creative team falls in love with a conceptual direction. The work looks stunning. The storytelling feels emotional. The typography feels elevated. The photography feels cinematic. The team becomes attached to the art rather than the outcome. Feedback challenging the work sounds like a threat. Positive reinforcement becomes proof the direction is genius. Confirmation bias wraps itself around the creative ego until story takes precedence over usability.

The rebrand suddenly demands a homepage experience unrelated to ordering. It demands menus reorganized around narrative rather than function. It demands digital transitions that slow down lines. It demands a loyalty program that fits a conceptual theme instead of behavioral truth. The system becomes contorted to serve the aesthetic rather than the guest. The brand believes it is building a world. The guest just wants a sandwich.

Cracker Barrel serves as a prime example of this dynamic in modern history. I was rather outspoken about Cracker Barrel's rebrand and evolution effort. I really didn't care much about the logo. The logo evolution was typographically sound. The rebrand missed the mark strategically. The company received data from sources like consulting agencies. They reinforced those findings to confirm a specific direction without looking at the counterpoint. That counterpoint was the core magic of the brand. Nostalgia drives Cracker Barrel. The company rolled out new prototypes and an identity that appeared to discard that nostalgia in favor of more youthful pastures. They sought relevance. They found alienation. The result was revolt because leadership confirmed the data they wanted to see while ignoring the emotional reality of their core guest.

Confirmation bias destroys problem solving. It convinces teams their long held assumptions are correct even when the world screams otherwise. Operations insists guests want more customization options. Tech insists guests want more automation. Marketing insists guests want more storytelling. Each department gathers data to prove their specific hammer is the solution to every nail. In the case of Cracker Barrel, the bias pointed to identity and interiors as the problem instead of food and service quality. Actual behavioral data showed the opposite. Guests want speed. Guests want clarity. Guests want predictability. But the team was already committed emotionally and politically. Confirmation bias closed the loop.

CX debt becomes permanent here. Tech debt becomes cultural. Operational strain becomes normalized. The organization builds systems to support the bias rather than the guest. Unwinding this requires immense political capital. Most leaders find it easier to press forward than to admit the foundation is flawed.

The Bias Loop operates as a system of self-reinforcing decisions rather than a one-time mistake. Survivorship bias tells you to copy the giants. Confirmation bias tells you that your decision to copy them is correct. They create a loop together that feels strategic. It feels data-driven. It feels safe. But it produces the exact opposite of clarity. It produces a hallucination of strategy that collapses the moment a real guest tries to place an order.

When Survivorship Bias and Confirmation Bias Collide

When these two biases join forces the result is a full-blown organizational pattern rather than a single flawed decision. A loop forms and continues until someone deliberately breaks it. The Bias Loop operates in silence. It manifests as hundreds of small and reasonable choices that accumulate over time until the brand experience becomes noisy and inconsistent. The operation becomes burdensome.

Here is the pattern.

A giant brand does something visible. They launch a feature or a flow. They debut a loyalty mechanic or a menu structure. The industry celebrates it. Blogs and analysts amplify the move. Teams hold it up as the future.

Survivorship bias proclaims that they succeeded because of this specific thing so we should do it too.

Leaders commit emotionally. The decision feels validated because a survivor did it. The team goes hunting for anything that proves the decision is sound. Usability tests get interpreted through a friendly lens. Customer complaints get rationalized. Operations challenges get reframed as temporary hurdles. Every red flag becomes a yellow one. Every yellow one turns green.

Confirmation bias insists that everything supports this direction.

The team proceeds. Implementation begins. The friction emerges slowly. No one wants to unwind the decision because the emotional commitment happened early. Reversing a decision feels like failure. Rethinking something feels wasteful. The loop tightens. The team adds more features to compensate for the flaws. They add more screens and more training. The product becomes heavier. The experience becomes slower. The operations team becomes more strained.

The next decision follows the same pattern because the Bias Loop remains unrecognized.

This quiet killer appears even before a restaurant brand enters the world. I have led the charge for over two hundred restaurant brand development projects. I have seen the Bias Loop in real life. I fell victim to it early in my career.

Founding restaurateurs often want to build the Chipotle of their specific cuisine. They aim to be the next Panera. This desire bleeds into the design where interiors and identities emulate the big players.

You see this play out in logo and interior design. Design school teachers showcase the top brands as examples of good design. Nike and Apple reign as supreme examples. Coca-Cola and Starbucks receive praise while observers disregard their design evolution over the decades.

This explains the resurgence of low-fidelity design. Crude illustrations and vintage style layouts have taken hold because high quality design signals corporate coldness. People latched on to the kitschy design styles because the vibe felt more human and tangible. The Bias Loop pushed designers into a world of emulating the macro brands while ignoring the effectiveness of more approachable design.

This loop explains why so many restaurant brands feel stuck. Their broken experiences stem from a decade of slightly biased decisions compounded by structure.

The Bias Loop persists because restaurant organizations unintentionally reward it. Leadership wants decisive action. Boards want to see innovation. Marketing wants to emulate category leaders. Technology wants to modernize. Operations wants tools that make life easier. Bias cares only about the paths of least resistance. Most brands lack the structure to challenge those biases meaningfully.

Restaurants end up with tech stacks too complex for their operational reality. They build digital experiences around conceptual aesthetics. They launch loyalty programs nobody understands. They create menu structures that require explanation. These outcomes happen because the system allows the Bias Loop to go unchallenged.

I once worked with a dessert concept poised for real digital growth. The brand had momentum. The team was energized. The early data validated the direction. First party digital sales climbed twenty eight percent after the first wave of improvements. That kind of gain signals that the system is working and the opportunity is bigger than leadership realizes.

Then the Bias Loop took over.

A private equity group stepped in and removed more than half the leadership team in a single week. No continuity plan existed. Transition knowledge disappeared. Alignment anchored in behavioral truth vanished. The new owners wanted a clean slate and an aggressive timeline. The people who understood the pulse of the business disappeared overnight.

The new leaders walked in with the kind of confidence you only see in people who have never touched the floor. They wanted a best in class tech stack because other brands used it. They wanted platforms with big logos attached. They wanted a consolidated vendor solution because the spreadsheets said it would be easier. They ignored the operational realities sitting beneath the brand. They ignored the signs of strain in the product model. They ignored the data that had already proven which tools the guests responded to.

Survivorship bias drove the decisions. Confirmation bias softened every warning.

Every concern was reframed as resistance. Every operational challenge was dismissed as executional. Every data point that contradicted their preferences was ignored.

They chased the brands they admired and assumed similar choices would produce similar outcomes. They treated context like an irritant. They treated evidence as optional. They treated digital strategy like a trend report.

The brand lost its tether to truth. The Bias Loop runs unchecked once truth disappears.

The new direction will collapse under its own weight because the architects never anchored it in the realities of the guest or the kitchens. It was anchored in the illusion that copying winners produces winning conditions. This is the story of how a brand with a twenty eight percent digital lift drifted backward because leadership trusted bias more than behavior.

This is the Bias Loop in its most expensive form. The loop becomes invisible when it goes unchallenged long enough. Invisible defaults create the quiet killers. Invisible killers create the broken experiences guests feel every day.

Case Study: Burger King Fights Dustiness with Mold

It is easy to confuse "Attention" with "Success." In the social media age, brands that make noise get applauded. They trend. They win awards. They get written up in AdWeek. For a restaurant leader watching from the sidelines, it is easy to assume that this noise equals growth.

Burger King spent nearly a decade trapped in this assumption. They fell victim to the Bias Loop in its purest form: looking at the visible tactics of "cool" brands, copying the noise, and ignoring the structural reality that actually drives revenue.

Chasing the wrong "Winner"

By the late 2010s, Burger King was lagging. McDonald's was winning on efficiency. Wendy's was winning on quality and a "snarky" social voice. Popeyes (a sister brand under RBI) broke the internet with the Chicken Sandwich.

Burger King leadership looked at these survivors and learned the wrong lesson. They succumbed to Survivorship Bias. They saw that Wendy's and Popeyes had massive cultural chatter, so they assumed chatter was the cause of the success. They missed the invisible reality: Popeyes succeeded because the sandwich was actually delicious. Wendy's succeeded because they had spent years upgrading their beef sourcing and store operations.

BK decided to copy the symptom (noise) rather than the cure (product).

Art Over Appetite

Burger King unleashed a torrent of "edgy" marketing. They let their "King" mascot appear in weird, unsettling skits. They trolled competitors on Twitter.

Then, in 2020, they launched the pièce de résistance: The Moldy Whopper. It was a high-definition, 45-second time-lapse of their signature burger rotting into a green, fuzzy mess. The strategic intent was to prove they had removed artificial preservatives. The creative execution was undeniable. It was bold. It was distinct.

The ad industry went wild. It won Gold Lions at Cannes. It generated billions of impressions.

The Confirmation Bias Trap

 Inside the BK boardroom, this looked like victory. Confirmation Bias took hold. The team looked for metrics that validated the strategy: "Look at the impressions! Look at the ad awards! We are culturally relevant again!"

They filtered out the metrics that contradicted the story.

Did it make people hungry? No. (Who wants to eat a rotten burger?)

Did it fix the speed of service? No.

Did it update the 1990s-era dining rooms? No.

While Marketing was popping champagne over awards, Operations was drowning.

Franchisees were dealing with aging equipment, complex menus, and slow drive-thrus. The brand perception was "cool ads," but the brand reality was "tired stores."

The Reality Check

The market eventually corrects every bias. While BK was winning awards, they were losing customers. By 2020, Wendy's officially surpassed Burger King to become the No. 2 burger chain in sales.

The buzz didn't convert because the Experience Chain was broken. The ads (Exploration) were interesting, but the store experience (Evaluation and Experience) was lacking. Guests would see a funny tweet, drive to a BK, and encounter a slow line and a dated lobby. The "cool" factor evaporated instantly.

The $400 Million Apology

In September 2022, Burger King essentially admitted the strategy failed. They announced "Reclaim the Flame," a massive $400 million corporate investment.

Notice where the money went. It didn't go to more stunts.

$250 million for "Royal Reset" (remodels and technology).

$120 million for advertising, but specifically advertising focused on quality and taste, not gimmicks.

Tom Curtis, President of Burger King North America, signaled the shift away from the Bias Loop: "We have to look like a modern restaurant, not a museum." They shifted from chasing viral moments to chasing operational excellence.

Takeaway

The Bias Loop tricked Burger King into playing a game of "Marketing" while their competitors were playing a game of "Operations."

Survivorship Bias made them copy the noise of competitors without the substance.

Confirmation Bias made them value ad awards over guest feedback.

Marketing can get a guest to the door once. Only the System can keep them coming back. If your ads are better than your burgers, you are not building a brand; you are building a disappointment.

CHAPTER 03
Quiet Killer 03: The Convenience Trap

Choosing Easy Over Effective and the Long-Term Cost of Short-Term Decisions

The Seductive Nature of "Easy"

Every restaurant brand eventually comes face-to-face with the same whisper: "Just do the easy thing." The whisper shows up in roadmapping and planning, store-level decisions, vendor meetings, and leadership conversations. It shows up after a quarter that ran too long or before a deadline that came too quickly. It shows up in brands that are growing and in brands that are struggling. It shows up because the restaurant industry is relentlessly demanding, and fatigue always makes convenience feel like the best path forward.

Quiet Killers 41

But the easy path isn't always wise. The easy choice can often be drift. And drift compounds the same way interest does. One shortcut becomes two. One workaround becomes a workflow. One tech system tacked on becomes a Frankenstein mess. One compromise becomes the new operating standard. And before a brand even knows it, the easy path has hardened into the only path akin to a narrowing alleyway that eventually dead-ends.

It's a structural killer that creates bigger, more expensive and taxing problems down the road. And it shows up in every layer of a restaurant brand's organization and system.

In operations, the convenience trap appears when teams build their own solutions to survive the day. Rearranging pickup zones, adjusting expo flow, reassigning labor dynamically, reorganizing prep because the digital system doesn't align with the kitchen reality. Operations becomes a patchwork of improvisations. What helped "today" becomes the SOP and a liability tomorrow.

In technology, the trap appears in the form of out-of-the-box platforms with rigid architectures, quick vendor installs, or bundled features that sound good in pitches but collapse under real behavior. These platforms impose someone else's logic onto your brand. They introduce someone else's menu architecture, someone else's modifier structure, someone else's kitchen sequencing, someone else's definition of a good user experience. The tech seems fast and cheap which may be true at first, but it becomes rapidly apparent that it's quite the opposite.

In marketing, the convenience trap appears as a dependence on campaigns to "fix" problems that are actually rooted in experience. Instead of solving the difficult structural issues behind low frequency or low conversion, marketing applies pressure where the system is already bending and pushes more guests into an experience that can't hold them. That pressure becomes strain. Strain becomes rework. Rework becomes cost.

In leadership, the convenience trap appears as the instinct to make short-term decisions because the quarter matters, because the board expects updates, because franchisees are frustrated, because the market is volatile. Leaders mean well. They choose easy because it feels responsive. But responsive leaders can still make regressive choices.

This instinct is so universal that McKinsey highlighted it in their 2023 work on operational complexity: "Organizations under pressure tend to prefer incremental fixes over systemic solutions, even when those fixes create greater long-term cost." They were describing enterprise retail, but the pattern maps perfectly to restaurants and arguably even more so, because restaurants operate under tighter margins, faster cycles, and more acute operational strain.

Restaurant brands live in urgency. Urgency creates shortcuts. Shortcuts create drift. Drift becomes dysfunction. Dysfunction becomes the quiet erosion of guest trust.

The convenience trap is not about laziness. It's about survival, or what feels like survival. But in a digital-first world, where the entire guest journey depends on clarity, predictability, and seamless operational execution, survival instincts often undermine the very systems the brand needs to build.

The irony is that the "hard path" isn't actually the hard path. It only feels harder at the beginning. Additionally, the hard path is almost assuredly a path to differentiation and competitive edge because so many brands refuse to choose it. Once a brand behaves with discipline, alignment, and clarity, everything becomes easier. Workloads become lighter. Decisions become faster. Conflicts become fewer. Systems stop fighting each other. And teams stop spending their lives reinventing bandages.

The convenience trap is a killer because it prevents this evolution. It keeps brands in reactive mode constantly sprinting, patching, compromising, and adjusting. It locks the organization into a pattern of solving the same problems repeatedly instead of solving the root problem once.

Restaurant brands cannot scale until they break the habits that keep them trapped in short-term thinking.

How Shortcuts Become Systems

Shortcuts would be harmless if they remained small. Workarounds would be benign if they truly expired. But fast-paced restaurant environments rarely allow temporary fixes to stay temporary. The moment a process functions even marginally well it enters the playbook. Teams repeat it. Trainers teach it. It solidifies into muscle memory. Muscle memory transforms a quick fix into a permanent system regardless of intentionality.

The Convenience Trap creates danger because shortcuts refuse to remain isolated. They snowball.

This phenomenon happens because the restaurant industry runs on adrenaline and immediacy. When a General Manager finds a way to bypass a clunky POS feature to get through a Friday night rush, they feel relief. They view the workaround as a victory. The brain records that victory. The next time the rush comes, the brain defaults to the workaround because the brain seeks the path of least cognitive resistance under stress. The workaround moves from an emergency maneuver to a standard operating procedure.

Consider the real world mechanics of this trap. A brand selects a quick-fix ordering system based on the promise of rapid deployment. The platform functions adequately for the first dozen locations. It handles the low volume without breaking. But the brand grows. Volume eventually increases and exposes critical limitations. Conflicting menu logic appears alongside rigid modifiers and confusing flows. Quote times become inconsistent while adaptability vanishes. The platform begins dictating operations rather than serving them.

McDonald's provides a concrete example of this phenomenon. They invested heavily in third-party digital solutions and acquisitions during the initial wave of kiosk innovation and digital transformation. They sought speed. They sought modernization. But they spent years reversing those choices after realizing that early decisions created technical debt across thousands of stores. Internal reporting quoted by CNBC in 2021 revealed that legacy digital structures slowed menu tests while complicating pickup workflows. The brand lost the ability to innovate quickly. Their response involved building new internal digital architecture and retraining the organization around unified systems. The cost of unwinding the shortcut was exponentially higher than the cost of building the right system initially.

Panera offers another case study. Their early mobile ordering nearly collapsed under peak usage because the digital promise of picking up in minutes was disconnected from operational capacity. They chose the path of launching fast with the intent to optimize later. They failed to acknowledge that optimization becomes nearly impossible once a system goes live across hundreds of locations. The operational reality of a sandwich line conflicts with the infinite capacity of a digital queue. The eventual fix required rethinking kitchen sequencing and labor choreography. Order routing needed a complete overhaul. The cost far exceeded what a slower and more systematic build would have required.

The Convenience Trap affects the most powerful restaurant brands on Earth without discrimination. Emerging brands are even more vulnerable if giants can get trapped. A small brand lacks the capital to rebuild its entire tech stack when the shortcut fails. The trap becomes a tomb.

Shortcuts solidify into systems through three specific mechanisms.

Repetition occurs first. Store teams simply repeat what worked yesterday. They do not analyze the long-term viability of the action. They care only that it solved the immediate friction.

Institutionalization follows. The repeated action becomes a default because no one challenges it. New hires watch the veterans use the workaround. They assume the workaround is the official process. The training manual says one thing while the culture does another. The shortcut becomes the culture.

Invisibility takes over last. The behavior is institutionalized so leadership stops seeing it as a problem. They see orders going out. They see revenue coming in. They do not see the friction or the wasted seconds or the cognitive load required to maintain the workaround. The inefficiency becomes invisible background noise.

Leaders frequently underestimate the compounded cost of shortcuts. Research from Bain & Company shows that companies operating with high organizational drag suffer significant productivity losses. Inefficiencies created by fast fixes and outdated processes cause them to operate at twenty to thirty percent lower productivity than their integrated counterparts.

Restaurants feel this intensity more acutely because operational drag manifests physically. It manifests in ticket times and throughput. It impacts digital conversion and labor stress while driving guest dissatisfaction. A workaround that adds ten seconds to an order seems trivial in isolation. Multiply that ten seconds by a thousand orders a day across fifty locations. You lose hundreds of hours of productivity every week. You lose revenue capacity. You burn out staff who have to fight the system to do their jobs.

Restaurants lose money by making fast choices that calcify into expensive permanent ones. They fail to look down the road to see what the future holds. They prioritize the relief of the present over the stability of the future. They choose the easy path because the hard path feels impossible when spinning a hundred plates constitutes a normal day.

Escaping the Convenience Trap requires a shift in leadership mindset. You must stop rewarding speed when speed creates debt. You must start rewarding clarity and scalability. You must recognize that a system is not just software. A system is behavior. If you build a system that encourages shortcuts you build a system designed to fail.

The Technology Trap

Restaurants denied their status as technology companies for decades. That denial is no longer sustainable. They are technology companies now. The Point of Sale sits at the center of the universe. Ordering platforms and loyalty systems orbit around it. Inventory tools and scheduling software dictate the rhythm of the shift. Kitchen Display Systems control the heartbeat of the line. Delivery integrations determine the reach of the brand. Customer Relationship Management platforms and personalization engines define the relationship with the guest. Operations run on code as much as they run on culinary execution.

This dependency makes technology the most dangerous place for shortcuts. The Technology Trap snaps shut the moment a leader prioritizes the speed of implementation over the flexibility of the architecture. It happens in the boardroom. It happens during the Request for Proposal process. It happens when exhaustion sets in and the leadership team just wants the problem to go away.

Vendors understand the pressure restaurant leaders face. They build sales decks to exploit it. They promise speed. They promise ease. They promise a turnkey solution that solves complex problems with a single contract signature. The phrase "we can launch you in six weeks" acts as a sedative to an organization under stress. It offers the illusion of a quick win. Brands say yes because they want the pain to stop. They want the problem solved. They want to move on to the next fire. They sign the contract believing they have solved a problem. They have actually purchased a cage.

Saying yes to easy technology creates long-term conditions that are nearly impossible to escape.

Technology is structural. It operates as a framework you live inside rather than an accessory you wear. Adopting a platform rewires the operational habits of the brand. It rewires the digital flows the guest relies on. It rewires the training protocols for every new hire. It rewires store-level expectations and manager workflows. It rewires customer behavior. Switching platforms resembles an organ transplant rather than a change of gloves. The body often rejects the new organ. The recovery time is long. The risk of failure is high. The cost of rejection is catastrophic.

Consequences multiply when a brand chooses a system because it was easy instead of right. The menu must conform to the database logic of the vendor. The user experience must conform to the template constraints of the provider. The loyalty logic must bow to the limitations of the backend. The operational flow must bend to match the software triggers. The brand evolves into a tenant inside someone else's building rather than the architect of its own destiny.

You cannot knock down walls in a rented apartment. You cannot innovate a guest experience inside a rigid tech stack. You cannot paint the walls a new color without asking for permission. Permission rarely comes because the vendor roadmap dictates your brand roadmap. You wait for features that never arrive. You apologize to guests for friction you cannot fix. You watch competitors innovate while you wait for a support ticket to clear.

Data confirms the high cost of these shortcuts. Gartner's 2022 Digital Commerce report found that sixty percent of brands that selected an out-of-the-box digital commerce platform replatformed within three years. They hit a wall. The constraints slowed product innovation. The system could not keep up with the strategy. The number is likely even higher for restaurants because digital commerce is tied directly to operational throughput. A retail store can survive a slow checkout process. A restaurant lunch rush cannot. Speed is the currency of the kitchen. A tech stack that lags steals revenue directly from the register.

The Convenience Trap persists because vendors know how to sell to exhausted teams. They know that speed sells. They know leadership craves a victory to show the board. They know that fractured organizations rarely challenge platform limitations during the sales cycle. The teams only find the walls once they are already living inside the house. The vendor incentive is lock-in. The brand incentive is flexibility. These goals are opposed.

The alternative path requires more discipline. It requires leaders to reject the allure of the quick fix. Brands that avoid the trap choose the harder path. They begin with behavioral truth. They align teams on the requirements before looking at vendors. They design the ideal flows intentionally. They select platforms based on flexibility rather than speed. They prioritize API connectivity over all-in-one promises. They demand access to their own data. They refuse to let a third-party logo sit between them and their guest.

This approach builds systems that scale. It avoids the expensive cycle of replatforming every thirty-six months. It prevents the drift that occurs when technology dictates operations. It empowers the operations team to control the flow of the kitchen. It honors guest behavior by building interfaces that match their intent. It creates momentum instead of constantly rebuilding it.

The restaurant brands that understand the Convenience Trap make technology choices that serve long-term flexibility. They realize that the easy choice today becomes the expensive choice tomorrow. They choose clarity over convenience because they have learned the cost of easy.

Breaking the trap requires a commitment to the hard work of clarity. Leaders must demand it across marketing. They must demand it across technology. They must demand it across operations. Clarity acts as the permanent antidote to the chaos of convenience.

The Hard Way Pays: How Chipotle's Discipline Became Its Advantage

The restaurant industry worships speed. Leaders celebrate fast launches and rapid pivots. They chase quick fixes. One of the most formidable restaurant brands of the last decade built its competitive edge by rejecting that impulse. Chipotle chose the hard path repeatedly and intentionally. They accepted friction in the short term to secure dominance in the long term. That discipline made the brand resilient. It made the brand formidable.

The allure of the Convenience Trap is strongest during a crisis. Chipotle faced an existential threat in 2015 following a series of food safety outbreaks. The easy path was obvious. Most brands would have launched a national apology tour. They would have flooded the market with heavy discounts to buy back traffic. They would have introduced menu novelties to distract the public. These moves are standard because they are fast. They create the appearance of action without requiring structural change.

Chipotle rejected the easy path. They chose to rebuild the entire operational foundation of the company.

On February 8, 2016, Chipotle closed every single location in the United States for a company-wide food safety meeting. This decision cost the company millions in lost revenue for a single day. It sent a signal that operations mattered more than transactions. They redesigned food safety protocols from the farm to the fork. They implemented high-resolution DNA-based testing of ingredients before those ingredients ever reached a restaurant. They rewired supplier relationships to ensure compliance. They slowed down the line to ensure safety.

The brand resisted the temptation to mask the crisis with marketing spin. They rebuilt trust through operational discipline. This is the hard way.

The strategy paid off. Reporting from The Wall Street Journal and CNBC confirmed that the recovery was not driven by a rebrand or a clever ad campaign. It was driven by operational rigor. CEO Brian Niccol emphasized this upon taking the helm in 2018. He stated that the comeback required integrating operations with digital platforms and hospitality to ensure the experience felt consistent everywhere. That sentiment captures the heart of avoiding the Convenience Trap. You fix the foundation before you paint the house.

The digital transformation at Chipotle provides the second and perhaps most significant example of choosing the hard way.

Most restaurant brands viewed digital ordering as an add-on channel in 2017 and 2018. They wanted to capture digital revenue without disrupting their core operations. The easy path was clear. Sign a contract with a third-party white-label provider. Bolt the software onto the existing POS. Let the vendor handle the roadmap.

Chipotle saw the future differently. They recognized that digital was not a channel. It was a behavior. Relying on a vendor meant renting their future. Chipotle made the difficult decision to build a fully custom digital ecosystem. They invested in proprietary ordering flows. They built backend logic that communicated directly with the kitchen.

This investment culminated in the Digital Make Line. This innovation fundamentally restructured how the back-of-house operates. Most fast-casual brands force digital orders down the same assembly line as in-store guests. This creates a bottleneck. The in-store guest watches the staff make burritos for invisible customers while the line stalls. The digital guest gets cold food because the kitchen is overwhelmed.

Chipotle built a second kitchen inside their kitchen. The Digital Make Line is a dedicated production station staffed by a separate crew that handles only digital orders. It requires more square footage. It requires more labor. It requires complex routing logic to ensure the right order goes to the right screen at the right time. It is expensive and operationally demanding.

It is also the engine of their dominance.

The Digital Make Line allowed Chipotle to scale volume without degrading the guest experience. It protected the throughput of the front line while uncapping the capacity of digital sales. The results are staggering. Chipotle's digital sales grew from approximately $200 million in 2016 to over $3.4 billion by 2022 according to public earnings reports. Digital sales accounted for nearly 40 percent of their total revenue. This surge happened because they built a system capable of handling the volume. They did not just add a button to a website. They re-architected the restaurant.

This infrastructure allowed for the Chipotlane. The brand realized they could leverage their digital engine to create a drive-thru experience that did not require a menu board or a speaker box. The Chipotlane is a pickup window for digital orders only. It increases new restaurant sales volumes and margins because it is purely accretive. It removes the friction of parking and entering the store. It works because the backend system is robust enough to predict exactly when the food will be ready.

Chipotle applied this same discipline to the rise of delivery aggregators. Most brands surrendered their data and margins to DoorDash and UberEats because it was the easy way to get delivery volume. Chipotle negotiated strict terms. They preserved control of their menu pricing. They used their massive loyalty base of over 24 million members to encourage direct ordering. They treated delivery as a feature of their own ecosystem rather than a service provided by someone else.

These were not glamorous decisions. They were operational and infrastructural choices. They required confidence and patience. They required saying no to the quick fix. They required alignment across marketing, digital, supply chain, and finance.

Chipotle proved that the hard way is only hard at the beginning. The easy way grows harder every year as a brand scales and the technical debt accumulates.

The company is not perfect. They face challenges like any major enterprise. Yet they stand as a rare modern example of choosing clarity over speed and integration over fragmentation. Their success did not come from viral campaigns. It came from system design. They rejected the Convenience Trap. They accepted the burden of building things right.

A brand that chooses the hard way early wins the easy way later. A brand that chooses the easy way early faces the hard way forever. Chipotle's story proves that clarity serves as the source of momentum.

Case Study: Wendy's Dynamic Pricing Punch

In the rush to adopt modern technology, brands often confuse capability with strategy. Just because a system can do something doesn't mean the brand should do it. Wendy's discovered this distinction the hard way in early 2024, when a single technical term uttered in an earnings call ignited a global PR crisis that threatened to undo decades of brand equity.

The Digital Gold Rush

By 2024, the "Digital Front Door" was the primary focus for every major QSR chain. Brands were investing billions in app infrastructure, loyalty engines, and digital menu boards. The goal was ostensibly better customer experience, but the underlying driver was margin optimization.

Wendy's was no exception. Newly appointed CEO Kirk Tanner touted a $20 million investment in high-tech digital menu boards for U.S. restaurants. These boards offered agility—the ability to change creative, update items, and adjust merchandising in real-time without the labor cost of swapping physical signage.

Optimizing Revenue, Ignoring Behavior

During an earnings call in February 2024, Tanner mentioned that this new tech stack would unlock "dynamic pricing and daypart offerings along with AI-enabled menu changes and suggestive selling."

To a room full of analysts and algorithms, "dynamic pricing" sounds like efficiency. It works for airlines. It works for Uber. It works for hotels. It is the convenient path to margin growth: let the computer adjust the price to match demand.

But to a human being buying a Baconator, "dynamic pricing" sounds like hostility.

The Surge Pricing Narrative

The reaction was immediate, visceral, and uncontrollable.

Consumers didn't hear "dynamic pricing" (a vague industry term). They heard "Surge Pricing" (a specific, painful consumer experience). The narrative spun out of control instantly: Wendy's is going to charge me more for lunch just because I'm hungry at noon.

Social media exploded. Senators called for investigations into price gouging. Competitors pounced—Burger King immediately launched a campaign offering free Whoppers, explicitly stating, "We don't believe in surging you when you're hungry."

Wendy's had walked into the Tech Trap. They allowed a feature of their hardware (real-time price adjustments) to dictate their public strategy. They ignored the fundamental behavioral truth of the restaurant category: Predictability is Trust.

When a guest drives to a QSR, they have a "reference price" in their head. They know roughly what a combo costs. If they arrive and that price has shifted because of an algorithm, the contract of trust is broken. The friction of wondering "Is it expensive right now?" destroys the habit loop.

The Walk-Back

Wendy's issued a clarification statement days later, frantically spinning the narrative. They claimed they never intended to raise prices during peaks, but only to offer discounts during slower dayparts. "We said dynamic pricing, we meant dynamic discounting."

Whether that was true or a pivot doesn't matter. The damage was done. The brand looked greedy. They looked like they were treating their guests as data points to be squeezed rather than people to be fed.

The Convenience Trap whispers that you should use every feature your tech stack offers. It tells you that automating revenue management is smart business.

But Wendy's proved that Guest Intent overrides Tech Capability.

The Tech allowed for variable pricing.

The Guest demanded consistent value.

Takeaway

An Integrated Organization would have vetted this "feature" against the Brand Clarity layer before ever mentioning it to Wall Street. They would have asked: "Does variable pricing reinforce our promise of 'Quality Is Our Recipe,' or does it erode trust?"

Technology must serve the experience, not the other way around. When you let the algorithm design the strategy, you lose the human.

CHAPTER 04

Quiet Killer 04: Siloed Leadership & Fragmented Execution

Why division amongst leadership is a recipe for failure

How Silos Formed in Restaurant Organizations And Why They Still Exist

Silos in restaurant organizations didn't appear overnight. They weren't created out of malice, incompetence, or political maneuvering. They formed because the industry grew up faster than its structures could adapt and each discipline built its own world in order to survive. Marketing built its world around campaigns and calendar-driven storytelling. Technology built its world around systems, uptime, integrations, and vendor contracts. Operations built its world around throughput, training, labor models, and daily firefighting. All three developed their own languages, their own KPIs, their own priorities. And over time, those priorities calcified into separate universes that orbit the brand without ever truly colliding.

In the early days of multi-unit growth, this separation made success possible. Units were opening fast. Franchises were scaling. The complexity of the category increased exponentially. Operations needed to be fiercely independent to maintain consistency across expanding footprints. Technology needed to adopt systems that could handle a higher volume of transactions and more intricate POS structures. Marketing needed to drive demand in an increasingly competitive marketplace. Each team had its own mission, and each mission felt urgent.

But urgency has a cost. When teams are forced to move quickly without shared foundations, they build their own frameworks for decision-making. Operations swears by efficiency. Marketing swears by creativity. Technology swears by stability. And once those frameworks harden, they rarely get revisited. Silos form the way coral reefs form: slowly, invisibly, layer by layer, until one day you realize you've built an entire ecosystem that is beautiful, intricate, and impossible to merge with anything around it.

As restaurant brands scaled, these silos got reinforced by incentives. Operations was measured by speed of service and accuracy. Marketing was measured by campaign lift and brand affinity. Technology was measured by uptime and reliability. None of these KPIs were wrong on their own, but together they created conflicting interpretations of what "success" meant. When three teams measure success differently, they naturally solve problems differently. And when they solve problems differently, the seams start showing in the guest experience.

Division and encampment became set in stone when brands hit an era of turbulent sales and growth. Sales decline became marketing's fault in the eyes of operations. Operational struggles were the villain from the perspective of others. Faulty tech, poor locations, bad employees, and on and on the culprits were identified while those who led those disciplines protected the choices with fervor.

And in many cases, everyone is right to blame and to defend. Because it is rare that slippage and declining sales is solely the problem of one department.

This is the core irony of restaurant silos: everyone is working hard, but they're not working toward the same experience. Marketing builds demand that digital can't fulfill. Digital builds flows that operations can't sustain. Operations builds workarounds that marketing never intended. The brand becomes a patchwork of interpretations: one version in ads, another in apps, another in stores.

The guest sees all three which culminates into perceived inauthenticity, confusion, and distrust The organization sees none of them.

Technology acceleration made the silos even deeper. As digital ordering and loyalty exploded, tech suddenly became a critical revenue engine. But legacy restaurant structures treated tech as a "support function" composed of a group that fixes what breaks and implements what the brand buys. As a result, tech often got brought in too late, asked to execute decisions it wasn't part of creating, or forced to stabilize systems built without a clear understanding of operational workflows.

If tech teams were tasked early with identifying new systems, it was for departments they didn't fully understand. They would struggle to gather requirements and take them at face value. Poll the industry for what the best players are using (notice the Bias Loop in play?), then go for the cheapest and easiest to implement. Oh look, the Convenience Trap!

Operations felt the weight of this immediately. They were the ones dealing with franchisees calling about tablet overload, drive-thru backlogs caused by confusing digital menu layouts, under-tested loyalty promotions that created line chaos, and POS updates that made Friday nights unpredictable. Silos always collapse onto the store. Always.

Meanwhile, marketing teams tasked with driving demand were often shielded from the operational consequences of its decisions. Campaigns would go live without verifying inventory realities. Digital messaging would push new items operations couldn't produce at speed. Loyalty would run "double points days" that overwhelmed kitchens. When it came to technology, marketing had a lot of room to make decisions because marketing tech didn't really affect other departments.

It wasn't intentional negligence. It was structural blindness. The system wasn't designed to force cross-functional accountability. Marketing, ops and tech didn't have a mechanism that required them to solve the same problem together.

Even today, the industry's structure reinforces silos. Annual planning happens in parallel. Tech has its roadmap. Marketing has its calendar. Operations has its staffing and training cycles. Each runs on its own rhythm, its own deadlines, its own operational heartbeat. Without integration, the brand behaves like a multi-headed animal trying to walk in different, opposing directions.

The most painful part is that none of this comes from incompetence. Restaurant leaders are some of the most capable people you'll ever meet. They're high-pressure decision makers who can solve problems in minutes with incomplete information. It's not leadership that's broken. It's the structure they inherited.

Silos are a foundational flaw, not a leadership flaw And like any foundational flaw, they only become visible under stress.

The last decade introduced exactly that stress. Digital ordering changed everything. Suddenly, marketing, tech, and operations weren't separate disciplines. They were three layers of the same experience. A marketing message on social media triggered a digital order. The digital order triggered an operational workflow. The quality of that workflow influenced the next digital order. The quality of that digital order influenced the next marketing outcome. The whole system looped back onto itself.

The funnel had already created friction. The Bias Loop had already fueled misguided decisions. The Convenience Trap created knee-jerk selections and decisions that hamstrung success. Silos are where those mistakes become embodied. They are felt physically in the store, digitally in the interface, emotionally in the guest.

Silos are not quiet because they hide. Silos are quiet because they are normalized. The industry has grown so used to them that leaders stop questioning how things should work and simply try to make the current structure work a little better. The problem is, you can't improve a structure that's misaligned at its foundation.

Silos need replacement. But before we get to replacement, we need to be brutally honest about what fragmented execution looks like in the real world.

The Three Versions of the Brand

Every restaurant brand believes it possesses one brand. One promise. One identity. One experience. Executives sit in boardrooms and nod in agreement over deck slides that outline a singular vision. Ask the guests and listen honestly to discover a different reality. They do not encounter one brand. They encounter multiple.

They encounter the brand according to Marketing. This is the crafted and polished expression of what the company wants the world to believe. This brand lives in campaigns and websites. It lives in social content and packaging. It lives in photography and tone of voice. Every Chief Marketing Officer can rattle off this version at dinner. It is strategic. It is emotional. It is elegant.

They encounter the brand according to Digital. This is the practical and functional reality of how the brand behaves online. This version lives in the app and the kiosk. It lives in the loyalty system and the ordering flow. It lives in the menu logic and search listings. This version is defined by code and constraints. It represents what the brand does rather than what the brand says.

They encounter the brand according to Operations. This is the lived manifestation shaped by staffing levels and equipment. It is defined by line flow and prep time. It is defined by pickup systems and throughput realities. This brand exists in the guest's hands. It exists in the guest's head and heart. Operations delivers the truth while Marketing delivers the dream.

The trouble begins when these three brands diverge. In most restaurant companies they diverge by default.

Marketing creates an aspirational brand focused on who the company wants to be. Digital creates a functional brand focused on what the company can currently execute. Operations creates a situational brand focused on what the company actually delivers under pressure.

Guests feel the gaps when these versions fail to match. They feel it when the digital promise clashes with the physical execution. They feel it when a promotion launches and operations cannot keep up because they were never briefed. They feel it when an app says an order will be ready in twelve minutes while the kitchen needs twenty-two. They feel it when the website speaks in polished brand language while the kiosk feels clumsy and mismatched. They feel it when loyalty promises value while the in-store process to redeem it is slow or confusing.

The guest does not know which department caused the inconsistency. They do not care. They only know the brand failed to keep its promise. The guest is always right about how the experience felt. Try telling them they are wrong. It will not end well.

Data supports the severity of this disconnect. Research from Harvard Business Review indicates that consistency is a far stronger driver of customer loyalty than delight. Brands that focus on consistency across all touchpoints see significantly higher revenue growth than those that focus on occasional moments of wow. A study by Price Waterhouse Cooper found that thirty-two percent of all customers would stop doing business with a brand they loved after just one bad experience. The stakes are absolute.

Marketing's version of the brand typically moves fastest. It evolves quickly. It responds to cultural shifts and new campaigns. It adapts to seasonal menus and category trends. It constantly refreshes itself to stay relevant. Marketing often builds this version in isolation. They define the aspiration without always understanding the constraints. They assume the system can handle the dream.

Digital's version moves slowest. This happens because technology is rigid rather than because digital teams lack creativity. Systems do not change on a dime. Vendors have roadmaps. Integrations have dependencies. UX improvements require research and validation. Digital must manage loyalty systems and POS integrations. They handle third-party data feeds and ADA compliance. Digital's brand is shaped by constraints marketing never sees.

Operations' version is the most honest. It is the most unforgiving. It is shaped by reality. Staffing shortages and equipment limitations define the day. Line backups and inventory issues dictate the pace. Training gaps and physical layouts constrain the flow. Marketing and Tech do not feel these pressures. Guests absolutely do. Operations does not get to imagine the brand. They have to deliver it.

Fragmentation begins the moment these three brands drift out of sync. It accelerates when no one feels responsible for reconciliation. It becomes visible when the guest feels the seams.

Consider the launch of a complex Limited Time Offer. Marketing dreams up a beautiful, multi-ingredient item that looks stunning on Instagram. They build a campaign around premium quality and craft. Digital builds a hero banner on the app to drive conversion. Operations realizes the item requires three new steps on the makeline during peak hours. The result is a disaster. The guest orders the beautiful item they saw online. They wait ten extra minutes because the kitchen is stalled. They receive a messy version of the product because the staff is rushing. The Marketing brand promised craft. The Operations brand delivered chaos.

This is a direct result of failed alignment.

McKinsey & Company has published extensive research on the value of omnichannel consistency. Their findings suggest that ensuring a seamless experience across digital and physical channels can increase customer satisfaction by up to twenty percent. The inverse is also true. Disjointed experiences degrade satisfaction rapidly. When a guest has to relearn the brand every time they switch channels, they eventually stop trying.

Teams defend their version of the brand instead of aligning around one. Fragmentation becomes the default state. Fragmentation is where the quiet killers do the most damage.

Leaders must recognize that these three versions exist. They must actively work to merge them. This requires empathy. Marketers must spend time on the line. Digital leaders must understand kitchen throughput. Operators must understand the digital roadmap. The goal is to create a single source of truth that accounts for the dream, the code, and the reality.

A unified brand is resilient. A fragmented brand is fragile. The work of leadership is to ensure the brand the guest meets in the ad is the same brand they meet in the app and the same brand they meet at the counter. Anything less is a broken promise.

What Fragmented Execution Looks Like and Why It's a

System Problem, Not a People Problem

If you want to understand the cost of siloed leadership, you don't look at strategy decks. You look at breakdowns. Real ones. The moments where the brand fractures in the guest's hands.

You see it when marketing launches a new LTO without confirming whether digital has updated the menu assets, or whether operations has enough prep labor to handle the spike. You see it when digital rolls out an ordering flow that reorganizes menu categories, only to have operations realize the new structure slows down expo stations. You see it when operations changes the in-store pickup flow to improve throughput, but digital isn't updated, so guests stand in the wrong place and get frustrated. You see it when loyalty updates create redemption confusion that frontline staff have to explain during Saturday rush.

Fragmentation is not theoretical. It's messy. And it always surfaces at the point of contact: the store or the guest's front door.

Nothing reveals fragmentation faster than a promotion. Marketing sees promotions as a megaphone. Operations sees promotions as a burden. Digital sees promotions as a logic puzzle. So you get a campaign that drives demand faster than operations can produce food. You get digital pathways that bury the promotional item four clicks deep because the information came late. You get store teams improvising because training didn't arrive in time, or because the promotion's actual workflow contradicts their staffing pattern.

The same fragmentation shows up in digital flows. Digital teams optimize for cognitive simplicity: shorter paths, fewer steps, cleaner menus. Operations optimizes for throughput: minimize kitchen chaos, maximize speed. Marketing optimizes for storytelling: seasonal pushes, brand personality, menu discovery. Tech optimizes for ease: out of the box systems that "natively integrate.". When these priorities collide, the flow becomes a compromise that satisfies no one and confuses everyone. A digital ordering flow should feel like one cohesive idea. Instead, it often feels like three conflicting philosophies fighting for control of the screen.

Loyalty fragmentation can be even worse. Marketing designs a points system shaped by emotional drivers. Digital implements it inside limitations no one realized existed. Operations trains the staff but quickly discovers redemption slows lines or requires awkward intervention from cashiers. Guests experience the entire dysfunction as brand inconsistency: "Why is it so hard to redeem this?" A brand's most powerful retention tool becomes a source of friction instead.

Pickup is another graveyard of fragmentation. Marketing pushes "fast and easy pickup." Digital sets pickup times based on optimistic prep algorithms. Operations has to reconcile both promises with labor, volume, and real-time chaos. The guest walks into the store expecting the brand promise. Instead, they encounter quick fixes created by divided departments and operational truth: this wasn't orchestrated to benefit them. And truth always wins.

When fragmentation is persistent enough, store teams begin to improvise. They create their own local workarounds. They reorganize pickup shelves. They bypass loyalty flows. They instruct customers to "just tell us your name next time." They post homemade signs. They modify POS entries. They skip complicated menu configurations. It's survival to the detriment of the brand. Operations compensates for organizational misalignment because they have no choice.

Fragmentation is even found in a department rarely talked about in these conversations: Finance. The fact is, finance holds a lot of the keys to open up innovation, marketing effectiveness, successful growth, and beyond. They also have the ability to systematically kill a brand's magic when they employ a myopic adherence to spreadsheet line items.

In this scenario, seen more and more as private equity takes the reins of multi-unit brands, finance gurus question every expenditure looking for efficiency. Innovation is often the first sacrifice to the efficiency gods especially with the short term and long term value cannot be easily explained or demonstrated.

Once value engineering endeavors start, they're hard to stop and the damage they cause is hard to reverse. It's experienced in the quality of the food as ingredients and vendors are squeezed. It's felt in the interactions with staff who are overworked and underpaid, but expected to smile as they hustle to eke out a living. It's seen in cheap technology solutions that check the box of utility without addressing the effects on the brand's overall experience or perception. And the people who feel it are the guests.

The fact is, guests don't care which department was responsible. Just as you care about ease and convenience in your role, they care about ease and convenience in their life. After all, you're a restaurant guest, too, at times.

And here's the real consequence: improvisation becomes culture.

When store teams must consistently fix what corporate creates, trust breaks. Corporate sees inconsistency. Operations sees disconnect. Digital sees workaround tickets. Marketing sees poor execution. But all of these symptoms point to the same root cause: fragmented leadership building fragmented systems that produce fragmented experiences.

This is why siloed leadership is not a people problem. It's not about ego, or communication issues, or departmental friction. It is a systemic problem born from outdated structures. The model itself is wrong. The incentives are misaligned. The rhythm of the work is mismatched. The KPIs are conflicting. The priorities are competing. And the guest is left to make sense of the contradiction.

The world where marketing, tech, and operations operate independently is gone. The guest collapsed that world the day digital and physical merged into one experience. The brand collapsed that world the day revenue shifted meaningfully into digital channels. The industry collapsed that world when third-party delivery rewired the definition of convenience. But the organizational structures remain unchanged for decades and still behave as if these worlds are separate.

The quiet killers thrive in those gaps.

They survive in the distance between teams.

They feed off the mismatches in priorities.

They grow in the absence of shared ownership.

To kill the quiet killers, the brand cannot simply "collaborate better." It must become something fundamentally different. Something integrated. Something behavioral. Something clear.

That shift begins in the next part of the book where we stop diagnosing the killers and start setting the record straight about how guests actually behave and what brands must truly deliver.

Case Study: Red Lobster's Endless Shrimp Debacle

Legacy brands often die slowly, but occasionally, they make a decision that accelerates the timeline so violently that the entire industry stops to watch. Red Lobster's decision to make "Ultimate Endless Shrimp" a permanent menu fixture in 2023 is one of those moments. It will be studied in business schools for decades, not just as a pricing error, but as a catastrophic failure of organizational integration.

On the surface, the move looked like a standard aggressive marketing play. Beneath the surface, it was a structural collapse caused by departments operating in completely different realities.

Desperation Breeds Disconnection

By 2023, Red Lobster was fighting for relevance. Traffic was softening. The casual dining sector was being squeezed by fast-casual competitors on one side and premium dining on the other. The brand needed a "traffic driver"—the holy grail of restaurant marketing departments.

In a siloed organization, when Marketing is tasked with "driving traffic," they look for the lever that pulls people through the door. They don't necessarily look at the P&L impact of that lever; that's Finance's job. They don't necessarily look at the table-turn time; that's Operations' job. They look at the offer.

"Ultimate Endless Shrimp" had been a successful Limited Time Offer (LTO) for years. It was a seasonal event that generated buzz and brought guests in once a year. The data from the LTOs likely showed high guest satisfaction and strong foot traffic.

Siloed Decision

Marketing made the call: Make it permanent. Make it $20.

In the Marketing silo, this was a home run. It was a clear, compelling value proposition that cut through the noise of inflation. It was an offer no competitor could match. It promised abundance in an era of "shrinkflation." The campaign launched with fanfare. The message was clear. The promise was bold.

But in an integrated organization, this decision would have triggered a "Launch Gate" review (as described in Chapter 11). Finance would have modeled the "mix"—the percentage of guests who would choose this specific item versus higher-margin entrees. Operations would have modeled the "dwell time"—how long a table sits when they are eating endless rounds of shrimp compared to a standard meal.

In a siloed organization, those conversations either didn't happen, or they happened too late to stop the train.

The Reality Check

The guest did exactly what the funnel predicted: they showed up. Traffic rose by 4 percent. In a vacuum, Marketing could have claimed victory. They hit their KPI. They drove demand.

But the restaurant does not live in a vacuum. It lives on a Balance Sheet.

The promotion triggered a behavioral shift the brand hadn't accounted for. Because the offer was permanent and cheap ($20), guests didn't treat it as a special occasion treat; they treated it as a challenge. They ate more shrimp per sitting than they did during the seasonal LTOs. They sat at tables longer, reducing the server's ability to turn the table and generate tips, which crushed morale.

More importantly, the price point was mathematically broken. The cost of the shrimp, combined with the volume consumed, meant Red Lobster was essentially paying guests to eat there.

The Collapse

The financial feedback loop hit hard and fast. In the third quarter of 2023 alone, Red Lobster posted an $11 million operating loss.

Ludovic Garnier, the CFO of Red Lobster's then-owner Thai Union, admitted the disconnect in a stark earnings call: "We knew the price was cheap, but the idea was to bring more traffic in the restaurants. So we wanted to boost our traffic, and it didn't work."

It didn't work because "Traffic" is a vanity metric if it doesn't convert to "Profit."

The Lesson Red Lobster didn't fail because they ran a discount. They failed because they allowed a department to optimize for a metric (Traffic) that actively destroyed the metrics of the wider system (Margin and Throughput).

This is the ultimate danger of Siloed Leadership.

Marketing succeeded: They got people in the door.

Operations failed: They couldn't turn tables profitably.

Finance failed: They bled cash on every check.

The Brand failed: It signaled desperation rather than value.

Takeaway

In an Integrated Organization, this promotion never would have launched at $20. Finance would have vetoed the margin structure. Operations would have flagged the table-turn risks. Marketing would have been forced to design a traffic driver that didn't cannibalize the core business.

Red Lobster's bankruptcy filing in 2024 wasn't caused solely by shrimp. But the Endless Shrimp debacle was the symptom that revealed the disease: a brand where the left hand didn't know, or didn't care, what the right hand was paying for.

Setting the Record Straight

The truth about modern behavior and what the brand must actually deliver.

The illusions are gone. We stripped away the funnel. We dismantled the bias loop. We exposed the convenience trap. You are now standing in the wreckage of the old way of doing things. It looks messy. It looks chaotic. It looks intimidating.

Good.

Now we can build something real.

Part II focuses on looking the guest in the eye and seeing them for who they actually are. They act as complex beings driven by ancient psychological needs and modern time constraints. They navigate a world drowning in noise. They search for a signal.

Your job is to become that signal.

This section explores the mechanics of modern choice. We will examine why confidence matters more than persuasion. We will look at how archetypes function as behavioral operating systems rather than creative costumes. We will define the specific ways a brand must behave to earn a place in the guest's life.

Brands are built on behavior. That behavior follows a pattern. Understanding that pattern stops the chaos and starts the predictability.

The time for excuses is over. The time for clarity has arrived.

CHAPTER 05

How Guests Actually Behave

The modern non-linear journey for today's guests

The Death of the Linear Journey and the Rise of Real Human Behavior

The first four chapters exposed the quiet killers. This chapter delivers the wake-up call that makes everything impossible to ignore. The biggest flaw in how restaurant brands think comes down to a simple truth. The guest journey does not exist. We built our plans and designs around a ghost. The linear path from awareness to consideration to purchase disappeared. We inherited it. We defended it. We repeated it for decades. It is gone.

Guests reject the funnel. They ignore predictable sequences. They refuse to narrow their choices slowly. Brand messages are no longer stepping stones to conversion. Guests behave like real humans living in a digital-first world where options are infinite. Attention is microscopic. Decisions happen in loops rather than lines.

This is an observable reality. You see it in the wild every single day. Guests discover a restaurant on social media. They look up reviews from strangers. They ask a friend if the food is good. They search the menu online and check travel time on Maps. They compare pickup windows across three brands. Then they switch to a completely different cuisine because a creator on TikTok reminded them of something else. They explore and evaluate. They abandon and reconsider. They choose based on confidence rather than persuasion.

Google proved this with their Messy Middle research. They studied thousands of real-world decision patterns and concluded that modern consumers do not progress toward a purchase. They circle around it. They bounce between exploration and evaluation. They repeat that loop until they feel confident enough to act. The brand with the most social cachet wins in the moment of choice. Certainty and clarity break the loop. Awareness fails to do so. Storytelling falls short. Persuasion misses the mark.

The Messy Middle depicts how guests behave in a restaurant context accurately because restaurants sit at the intersection of convenience and habit. Proximity and emotion play a role alongside social influence. No category is more susceptible to nonlinear behavior. No category switches faster. No category suffers more from assuming the old model still works.

Most restaurant leaders misinterpret the Messy Middle as a Gen Z phenomenon. It is a human phenomenon accelerated by technology and the rapid adoption of digital channels during the Pandemic of 2020. Gen Z is native to loops. They grew up in them and navigate them effortlessly. Millennials loop too. Gen X loops. Boomers loop. Anyone with a smartphone and a hunger pang loops. The cognitive pattern is universal while the speed of the loop varies. The idea that younger guests behave differently is a distraction. All guests behave differently now. Digital culture changed human behavior rather than just youth behavior.

BCG's influence map confirms this. Their research found that the most powerful drivers of choice sit in the middle of the journey. Social proof and proximity matter more than awareness triggers. Convenience and reviews drive decisions alongside perceived value and brand familiarity. The battle for restaurant choice is won or lost long before a guest ever reaches your website or kiosk.

Archrival's work reinforces the same pattern. Their insight shows that Gen Z exposes the truth the rest of us ignored. They switch fluidly. They abandon apps easily to manage valuable space on their devices. They trust peers over brands because brands have proven themselves to be bad actors with regard to their values. They use infinite-choice environments as second nature. Their patterns reflect the new baseline for decision-making across all demographics. Gen Z simply behaves openly in a way the rest of us do privately.

Brands must stop using generational stereotypes as an excuse and start examining universal behavior. They would see the writing on the wall. The linear model fails to map to reality. The divergence is too extreme to ignore.

This mismatch explains why so many restaurant digital experiences feel out of sync. They greet guests as if they just arrived at the top of a funnel. Those guests actually arrive forty steps into their decision carrying context the brand cannot see. Marketers treat the website like an awareness builder even though the guest is there to complete the order. They treat the app like an engagement platform while the guest uses it as a tool. They treat loyalty like a storytelling channel while the guest needs it to reinforce clarity and value.

Third party delivery and aggregator brands like DoorDash and UberEats have sniped massive amounts of business for this reason. They deliver a predictable and easy to use experience in a singular app. A guest may lose out on the opportunity to collect points. Who cares when the value of said points lacks clarity or the trade off fails to impress?

Blind dedication to funnel led thinking hides this reality. It leads marketers down a path of bigger offerings and more storytelling on digital channels. It creates more options. Your guest lacks curiosity about your brand when they land on your site. The funnel assumes curiosity. The Messy Middle presumes intent. That difference changes everything.

Guests want respect when they reach a digital touchpoint. They want speed rather than story. They want clarity rather than choreography. They want the shortest distance between hunger and satisfaction. Any brand that forces them to move deeper into the brand misunderstands the assignment. The role of the brand is to eliminate friction at the decisive moment in a nonlinear world.

The same truth applies to physical experiences. Blocking the approach to ordering and egress is insane. Forcing guests to enter through multiple marketing doors just to get in the building is idiotic. Relegating ordering to a separate building is a disaster. Yet brands continue to create new ways of approach and egress inside the four walls.

Fresh 2 Order based in Atlanta serves as an example. The food is great even though the menu has remained the same for nearly 20 years. Entering a location feels different. The approach is wide open directly in front of the doors. No right or left turns exist. You do not have to look for the queue. Ordering is easy. The friction happens afterward. Turning left or right is unclear. The fountain drinks are to the right. You have to cut through the right lane if you are in the left ordering area. Waiting areas are undefined. Leaving requires cutting through tightly spaced tables with dining guests. You successfully interrupt their meal. It creates a bad experience for everyone.

Forward-thinking restaurant brands are quietly reorienting themselves around behavioral truth rather than marketing myth. Look closely to see the signs. Menu categories are being restructured around cognitive shortcuts. Ordering flows are being stripped of nonessential screens. Pickup areas are being redesigned around clarity and visibility. Brand messaging is being slimmed down at critical stages. Loyalty is being simplified to remove guesswork. Personalization is being used to reduce decision fatigue instead of inflating options.

This is behavioral alignment put to work. It builds clarity. A brand decides to meet guests where they are rather than where the funnel imagined them to be.

The modern journey acts as a storm rather than a funnel. Your brand controls the shelter rather than the wind.

Everything that comes next in this book builds on this foundation. Brand clarity and UX strategy rely on it. Data discipline and operational integration require it. Every strategy you build will be a degree off if you do not accept nonlinear behavior as the operating reality. Every degree off compounds as you scale.

Understanding the Messy Middle means abandoning the illusion of controlling a nonexistent linear path. It means adopting a new model. A new path must be pioneered because controlling the linear journey is dead. Clarity sits at the core of that path. Clarity is the new superpower.

We will flatten the old model entirely in the next subsection. We will drill deeper into the behavioral forces that drive real restaurant decisions. We will see how psychological and environmental forces collide in ways no linear framework can possibly account for.

Why Guests Arrive With Intent, Not Curiosity

By the time a guest reaches your digital front door, they are ending a journey. Every tap, scroll, search, and glance before that moment shaped their intention. They compared options. They evaluated value. They made micro decisions triggered by habit, impulse, proximity, or the opinion of a stranger. Restaurants often imagine their website or app as the first chapter of the story. For the guest, it serves as the epilogue.

Intent remains the most misunderstood force in the modern restaurant world. Leaders still behave as if the guest is gently warming up to the brand. They imagine the customer gathering information like a student preparing for a test. That assumption creates digital experiences bloated with persuasion. Apps become cluttered with unnecessary context. Websites overflow with campaigns and storytelling that feel meaningful internally yet remain irrelevant externally. Intent renders all of that obsolete.

Google's Messy Middle research makes this explicit. The moment a customer clicks through to your domain marks the end of their evaluation. They simply want to complete the task. Confidence breaks the loop. That moment requires nothing from the brand except clarity, speed, accuracy, and execution.

Psychologists refer to this shift as the transition from a deliberative mindset to an implemental mindset. During the deliberative phase, the brain remains open to new information. It weighs pros and cons. Once the brain crosses the threshold into the implemental phase, it closes off to new data. It focuses entirely on execution. When a restaurant brand interrupts this execution phase with marketing messages or "brand storytelling," it forces the brain to reopen a closed loop. This causes cognitive strain. The guest experiences this strain as frustration.

Restaurants tend to overestimate how much guests want from them while underestimating how much guests expect from them. A guest refuses to sacrifice a predictable pathway for a personalized greeting. They reject an immersive story if a clunky route to an inaccurate order follows it. They do not want discovery features. They want cognitive shortcuts. They would have browsed before arriving at your physical or digital experience if they wanted to browse. They would have stayed on social media if they wanted inspiration. They would have never left the review sites if they wanted to explore.

Intent is focused. Intent creates the most valuable state a guest can be in. Yet most restaurant brands treat intent as if it needs nurturing. They act as if the guest still needs convincing. That serves as the outdated funnel whispering in the background. Intent requires alignment rather than persuasion.

This mismatch becomes painfully obvious when you observe real-world behavior. Watch someone order Starbucks from their phone while in line at Target. They lack a reflective or leisure mindset. They operate efficiently. They run a micro mission. They match hunger with convenience while juggling three other things in life. Their intention is sharp. Any friction increases the chance they switch to the brand with a clearer path. That switch represents cognitive conservation rather than emotional betrayal.

Biology plays a role here too. The hungry brain has less patience for ambiguity. Decision fatigue sets in quickly when blood sugar drops. Research from the National Academy of Sciences suggests that decision quality deteriorates as the brain runs low on glucose. A complex menu or a disruptive pop-up demands energy the guest does not have. The brain interprets this complexity as a threat. It seeks to escape the threat.

BCG's research found that eighty percent of consumers use shortcuts to accelerate decision making. This holds particularly true in restaurants where the stakes are low and the options are abundant. A guest refuses to compare ten menu categories. They want to recognize something familiar fast. They refuse to scroll through thirty modifiers. They want the most common combination served instantly. Behavior determines the moment.

Intent also explains why brand story lacks the influence marketers imagine. Guests simply do not need your brand story at the moment of action. There is a time and place for that. Story shapes memory. Storytelling belongs where the guest intends to receive it such as social media. Intent shapes behavior. That distinction matters. Restaurants often inject their story into the wrong part of the journey. This dilutes the clarity guests need at critical moments. Let narrative shape affinity. Let utility shape conversion.

Intent changes everything about how physical spaces, digital ordering, loyalty, and menu design should work. A digital home creates tension if it treats guests like they are early in the process. It creates flow if it treats them like they are late in the process. The challenge lies in accepting that your brand plays a supporting role in the moment. The guest plays the hero.

This is the humility the modern journey demands. You must recognize that the brand acts as a tool in the guest's life rather than the center of it.

The faster restaurant teams accept that the guest arrives with clarity, the faster they can design experiences that match reality. Intent is not something to shape. It is something to honor.

We must now go deeper into the actual mechanics of what precedes intent. We will examine the loops, shortcuts, heuristics, and influence webs that shape decisions long before brands even notice the guest exists.

Untangling Google's Messy Middle

Google's Messy Middle research revealed what behavioral psychologists have understood for decades. Human decision making is rarely linear. It operates as a continuous loop of expanding and contracting options. This cycle of exploration and evaluation continues until the individual feels confident enough to commit or reaches a physical tipping point like hunger.

Exploration acts as the moment of possibility. A guest opens Instagram and sees a video of Korean corn dogs. They save it. They think about it. They share it with a friend. Then they open Maps and search for "corn dog near me" even though they had no plans to eat corn dogs that morning. Exploration is curiosity fueled by algorithms. It is driven by proximity, habit, cravings, and peer influence. It creates a mental list of "what if."

Evaluation acts as the moment of discernment. The guest compares star ratings. They check photos to see if the food looks like the ads. They look at menus to see if the price matches the value. They scan wait times. They skim comments for red flags. They ask someone nearby if they have tried it. They weigh convenience against desire. They calculate the cognitive cost of trying something new versus the safety of the familiar. This evaluation is not formal analysis. It is rapid-fire, subconscious, pattern-recognizing decision making.

The loop forms when these two mental states collide. Exploration triggers evaluation. Evaluation triggers more exploration. A guest explores Korean corn dogs, evaluates the drive time, decides it is too far, and jumps to poke. They evaluate the poke spot, realize they had fish yesterday, and return to burgers because burgers are familiar and fast. That loop can last twenty minutes or twenty seconds.

This loop happens in seconds at the moment of truth just as often as it happens slowly during day-to-day activities. Guests doomscroll while not actively thinking about food, yet your brand appears in the feed. They check the box of exploration. A guest drives to run errands and sees your signage. They check the box of exploration. They end up in a meeting where a coworker mentions your brand. That is evaluation in motion.

These moments compound and collect every minute of every day. Every interaction with your brand that supports your purpose and promise adds another reason to believe. Every interaction that detracts from that purpose reduces confidence and interest.

I like to think of this as a metaphoric fire.

Every time you support the grand purpose and promises of the brand, you throw wood on the fire. A great social post is a twig. A seamless ordering experience is a log. A consistent operational execution across ten visits is a giant tree. The fire gets bigger. It gets hotter. It becomes a beacon that is hard to ignore.

When a brand creates uncertainty or muddies the clarity, they throw water on the fire. Small inconsistencies act like a cup of water. It sizzles, but the fire survives. Larger issues act like a firehose. A rude staff member, a crashed app, or a hidden fee extinguishes the guest's intent instantly. The loop relies on building that fire as big as possible throughout every single interaction. There are no workarounds. There are no exceptions.

Restaurants mistakenly believe they can break the loop through persuasion. The Messy Middle makes clear that persuasion is weak compared to shortcuts. People rely on heuristics. These are simple mental rules used to speed up decisions and conserve energy.

Closest wins. Fastest pickup wins. Highest rating wins. Most familiar wins. Most value wins.

These shortcuts are not logic-based. They are survival-based. They conserve cognitive effort. The brain wants to burn as few calories as possible when making a low-stakes decision like lunch.

The loop explains why guests bounce between channels. They might search on Google, switch to TikTok to see videos, hop to Yelp for reviews, jump to Maps for proximity, then click into your website to confirm menu options. This behavior represents efficiency rather than disloyalty. The guest is assembling a complete picture of confidence using the best tool for each specific piece of data.

Archrival's research into younger consumers showed the same thing. The modern mind is highly adaptive rather than chaotic. Switching is about optimization of time and resources. Younger consumers are simply better trained in the loop because they grew up in infinite-choice environments. The pattern exists across generations. A Boomer compares reviews as aggressively as a twenty-two-year-old. A Gen X parent checks pickup times as compulsively as a college student. Millennial parents use heuristics like experts. The behavior is universal. Only the speed varies.

The loop is emotional. Mood, stress, time pressure, and social context shape decisions almost as much as price and proximity. People do not choose restaurants rationally. They choose restaurants relative to their physical, emotional, and logistical state. The funnel never accounted for this. The Messy Middle reveals it perfectly.

Here lies the most important insight the loop brings to restaurant brands. By the time a guest reaches your brand's doorstep, whether digital or physical, they have already completed dozens of micro-evaluations you did not see. Your job is not to recreate the process they already finished. Your job is to avoid undoing it.

A slow load time? Loop undone. Long drive-thru line? Loop undone. A cluttered homepage? Loop undone. Confusing menu categories? Loop undone. Forced login? Loop undone. Pickup times that feel unrealistic? Loop undone. A surprise fee? Loop obliterated. Slow make times? Loop undone. Rude staff? Loop undone.

The Messy Middle is generous in possibility but ruthless in execution. It allows guests to consider you many times. It gives you only one chance to deliver at the moment of action.

Now that we have dissected the loop, we need to contextualize it for restaurants specifically. No category is more susceptible to environmental, operational, and contextual influence than food.

The Unique Volatility of the Restaurant Decision Loop

If the Messy Middle applies universally, it explodes inside restaurants. This category faces hyper-nonlinear behavior at a scale like no other. The stakes feel low financially but high emotionally and logistically. Guests make decisions under pressure. They make decisions while multitasking. They make decisions socially by asking what the group wants. They make decisions emotionally based on cravings. They make decisions logistically based on time constraints. They make decisions financially based on perceived value. They make decisions out of habit. They make decisions emergently based on speed. All of these decisions happen faster than most brands assume. They occur under constraints the funnel never accounted for.

Biology plays a significant role here. A hungry human behaves differently than a shopper buying insurance or shoes. Hunger creates a biological urgency that sharpens focus and lowers patience. The brain seeks the fastest route to satisfaction. It filters out noise aggressively. This reality transforms the Messy Middle from a leisurely loop of exploration into a high-speed race for resolution.

Restaurants are chosen under time pressure more than any other consumer category. McKinsey's work on choice architecture has consistently shown that short decision windows increase reliance on heuristics. These short windows decrease the impact of persuasion. That data lines up perfectly with BCG's findings showing proximity, value, convenience, and familiarity as top drivers for fast casual and QSR selection.

People reject more options despite the prevailing belief among many restaurant leaders that variety drives traffic. They want fewer decisions. They want to streamline and simplify their decision time. The cognitive load of choosing between fifty items is a barrier. The ease of choosing between five items is a relief.

Raising Cane's serves as a fantastic example of this dynamic at play. Talk to a majority of restaurant leaders and aspiring restaurateurs. They are awestruck by Cane's. They ask how a brand selling only chicken fingers got so big and successful with such a basic offering. The answer is simplicity and clarity. Their offering is easy to categorize. Purchasing the food is easy to do. The fingers are great to those who love the brand. It takes almost no effort for guests to adopt Cane's into their weekly habits and routine. The brand removed the burden of choice. They replaced it with the comfort of certainty.

This explains why the majority of restaurant choices are habitual. Habit represents efficiency rather than laziness. Habit is a pre-solved loop. Once a guest gains confidence in a brand's consistency, speed, and predictability, they stop exploring. They jump straight to evaluation and pick the option that feels safe. Behavioral economics calls this a default behavior. Restaurants experience it as repeat business.

The brain loves default behaviors because they conserve energy. When a guest knows exactly what they will get, exactly how long it will take, and exactly how it will taste, the risk of disappointment drops to near zero. That psychological safety is more valuable than a new menu item or a clever marketing campaign.

But restaurants lose habitual customers constantly because their digital or physical execution breaks the loop. The category is unforgiving. One bad pickup experience erases five good ones. One slow Saturday reroutes a family for six months. One confusing kiosk flow nudges someone to a competitor forever. The habit is fragile. It relies on the brand keeping its operational promise every single time. When the brand breaks that promise, the guest is forced back into the exploration phase of the Messy Middle. They are forced to look for a new default.

Add third-party delivery into the mix and the journey becomes even messier. The loop expands to include aggregators who care about their own conversion rates rather than your brand loyalty. Guests compare delivery times dynamically. They weigh surge pricing. They toggle between apps to find the fastest or cheapest window. Loyalty points, promotions, delivery fees, distance, and restaurant readiness all collide in a single decision. That decision flips multiple times in seconds. The brand is often just a thumbnail in a list of infinite options. The only thing that secures the order in that chaotic environment is the guest's confidence that your food will arrive hot and correct.

The industry's biggest mistake lies in believing the guest wants more "brand" in these moments. They do not. They want less friction. They want to trust a brand's claims. They want clarity in the offering. They want reliability. They want predictability. They want confidence that the meal will arrive on time, correctly packaged, correctly prepared, and without unnecessary steps.

Brands often try to compensate for operational complexity with storytelling. They try to mask friction with personality. This fails because the guest is not looking for a friend. They are looking for a solution. When a brand prioritizes narrative over utility during the ordering process, they signal that they do not understand the guest's needs.

This is why the next chapter, Brand Clarity, serves as the undeniable foundation. Behavior becomes unpredictable without clarity. Decisions become inconsistent without clarity. The brand becomes fragmented without clarity. Fragmentation kills in a nonlinear world.

Restaurant brands cannot afford to optimize for imagination. They must optimize for how humans actually behave. They must respect the loop. They must honor the intent. They must build systems that support the shortcuts guests use to survive the day.

The loop is real. Intent is real. Behavioral shortcuts are real. Acknowledge these truths and the rest of the book becomes a blueprint rather than an argument. You are ready to build a brand that works with the human brain rather than against it.

CHAPTER 06
Brand Clarity

Introducing the cure to the quiet killer chaos

What Brand Clarity Actually Is And Why Most Brands Are Lacking It

Let's start by establishing the nature of Brand Clarity. It extends far beyond creativity or storytelling. It functions deeper than a manifesto, a mood board, or a tagline. Clarity exists as the brand a guest recognizes without thinking. It serves as the simplest, sharpest articulation of what a brand is, what it does, and the specific problem it exists to solve in the guest's life.

The modern restaurant world often complicates clarity. Clarity is the opposite of complication. It remains when you strip away everything unnecessary. It represents the brand in its purest, most practical form. It stands as the competitive advantage that magnifies every other advantage a brand possesses.

Quiet Killers

Most restaurant brands fail because they lack clarity rather than creativity. Failure happens when no one can articulate the core reason for existing without slipping into poetic language that sounds pretty but fails to connect. Failure occurs when marketing imagines the brand one way while operations experiences it another way and technology represents it a third way. Without clarity, every decision becomes a gamble. Every department becomes its own lighthouse guiding the ship in different directions.

Clarity is alignment. Clarity is direction. Clarity is consistency. Clarity is trust.

A guest requires a recognizable and dependable brand rather than a clever one. The brain relaxes when a guest can predict exactly what the experience will feel like. This prediction covers the food, the ordering flow, the pickup process, the value equation, and the environmental cues. Once the brain relaxes, the loop breaks. The brand earns the behavioral equivalent of loyalty when the loop breaks.

Psychologists call this Cognitive Fluency. It is the measure of how easy it is for our brains to process information. Research consistently shows that people prefer things that are easy to think about. When a brand is high-fluency, the brain interprets that ease as truth, safety, and value. When a brand is low-fluency—confusing, inconsistent, or cluttered—the brain interprets it as risky. Clarity is not just an aesthetic decision. It is a biological trigger for trust.

Most restaurant brands mistakenly treat "brand" as a layer of flavor sprinkled on top of the real business. They treat brand as something the marketing team owns. They express it on Instagram, on packaging, in tone of voice, and in campaigns. Brand lives in decisions rather than language. Brand is how you behave and what that behavior builds within guests.

The brands with the strongest clarity do not always possess the prettiest identity. They possess the most consistent identity. They have the most legible purpose. They deliver the most predictable experience. Walk into Chick-fil-A, In-N-Out, Raising Cane's, or Sweetgreen to feel clarity in the bones of the business. You feel it in the simplicity of the menu and the vocabulary. You see it in the operations and the digital systems. It appears in the training and the pickup shelving. It manifests in the way each team member interacts with the guest. The experience is defined rather than just designed.

Clarity defines what a brand knows and what a brand refuses.

A brand with clarity knows exactly who it serves. It knows exactly who it does not serve. It knows what problem it solves. It knows which problems it ignores. It knows which features matter. It knows which ones are vanity. It knows which tech it needs. It knows which tech serves as a distraction. It knows what to say yes to. More importantly, it knows what to say no to.

Purpose means the problem you solve in the life of your guest in this context. It is nothing more and nothing less. Purpose is utility. Purpose is dependability. Purpose is behavioral alignment. The advertising and marketing industry wrongly confused Purpose for moral performance over the last decade. Every brand felt pressure to stand for something bigger. "Bigger" encouraged brands to color outside the lines of their core focus.

Some brands have created a believable dedication to something bigger. Tying that bigger principle back to the food drives success. Chipotle serves as the prime example with their dedication to responsible food sourcing and cleaner eating. This is bigger than just making burritos and burrito bowls. That bigger ideal has downstream effects on the perceived quality of the product. The influence is symbiotic and clear despite the bigger picture purpose.

Firehouse Subs provides a different example with their alignment with local fire departments. The connection makes sense because of the founders' firefighting history. This alignment does little to influence the quality of product or service. It serves as a bonus that sits separate from the core offering. That is effective in its own right, yet it lacks the power of a product-related Purpose.

Guests require uniqueness in offering to be clear. They require the bigger purpose to have a clear positive effect on the food and service itself. Big is optional. Clear is mandatory.

The simplest brands win because they remove friction. The most consistent brands win because they reinforce expectation. The clearest brands win because they reduce cognitive effort. Clarity becomes a shortcut in a nonlinear world full of infinite choice. A guest waits to weigh your brand against competitors until the choices have been reduced to the brands that feel easiest.

The absence of clarity rarely looks like chaos. It looks like small inconsistencies. A menu fails to match the brand's focus. A digital flow contradicts in-store operations. A tone of voice shifts between the website and the app. A loyalty program conflicts with the value equation. A seasonal item breaks the promise. Clarity fails slowly. It is overlooked or tolerated as temporary until it fails all at once.

How Clarity Shapes Every Department's Decisions

When a brand possesses clarity, every department aligns. Marketing knows exactly what message to amplify. Technology knows precisely which systems to build. Operations knows which processes to enforce without hesitation. Finance understands which investments defend the core value proposition. Clarity acts as infrastructure. It serves as a filter. It becomes the rules of engagement for the entire company.

When clarity is missing, departments compensate. They invent their own interpretations of the brand and devise their own methods to reach goals. They reverse-engineer meaning based on their specific KPIs. They fill in the blanks from their own biased perspectives. They make decisions based on preference instead of direction. This is where fragmentation begins.

Marketing, without clarity, becomes theatrical. It chases attention rather than connection. The team launches campaigns that win awards but fail to drive traffic. They write copy that sounds poetic but communicates nothing about the food. They prioritize "brand love" over brand utility. They mistake noise for signal.

Technology, without clarity, becomes mechanical. It solves for specs rather than people. The tech team buys platforms because they look good on a feature matrix, not because they solve a guest problem. They build complex loyalty integrations that slow down the checkout flow. They optimize for backend stability while sacrificing frontend usability. They treat the guest as a user ID rather than a human being with a hunger pang.

Operations, without clarity, becomes improvisational. The kitchen invents workarounds because the official process is too slow. Managers make judgment calls that contradict corporate policy because corporate policy contradicts reality. Training becomes a game of telephone where the standard degrades with every new hire. The experience varies from shift to shift and store to store.

Finance, without clarity, becomes myopically protective. They see every line item as a cost to be cut rather than value to be preserved. They slash labor hours to hit a quarterly target, ignoring the downstream impact on speed of service. They cheapen ingredients to save pennies, eroding the very quality that brings guests back. They become the formidable brick wall standing in the way of progress rather than the fuel for it.

These four departments drift away from one another as they individually build their own definition of the brand. They deliver actions, approaches, and decisions with varying degrees of distance from the core truth. The differences compound. Guests get lost in the gap between what Marketing promised, what Tech built, and what Ops delivered. Loyalty evaporates because of a thousand small failures, inconsistencies, and a track record of confusion.

Clarity eliminates that drift.

Marketing becomes sharper because it no longer projects what is cool. Instead, it communicates what is true. When clarity is present, marketing stops chasing trends and starts reinforcing expectations. Teams find it easier to identify opportunities to connect rather than striving for the next viral craze. Clarity trims the fat from campaigns. It removes narrative fluff because it forces marketing to adopt behavioral logic. It turns messaging from creativity for the sake of it into performance, utility, and unique brand experience. The goal shifts from "get them to look" to "help them decide."

Technology becomes smarter because clarity removes unnecessary features. A brand that knows its purpose does not need fifty bells and whistles. It needs five that work flawlessly. Clarity stops teams from buying the wrong platforms, integrating the wrong tools, and choosing systems that look impressive in demos but fall apart in operations. It prevents the accumulation of technical debt by forcing every tool to justify its existence against the guest experience. Clarity is the difference between a scalable tech stack and a Frankenstein monster stitched together by vendors with competing roadmaps.

Operations becomes consistent because clarity creates rules. It sets the experience standard. It defines sequencing. It simplifies training. It removes the gray area frontline teams constantly battle. Clarity lets operations say, "This is the way," not from ego but from alignment. Store teams no longer have to improvise because the brand has already defined the right way. When the menu is clear, the prep is clear. When the promise is clear, the speed is clear. Operations stops being the department where good ideas go to die and becomes the department where the brand actually lives.

Finance becomes aligned because clarity gives them an understanding of the value of opportunity. It defines investments instead of costs. It empowers bigger picture thinking for long term success rather than short term savings. It enables finance to sit at the table as a strategic partner. They understand why spending money on a custom digital ordering flow protects revenue rather than just consuming capital. They understand why labor investment drives throughput. The organization thrives with intelligent, data-driven, and brand-clarity-backed progress as a result.

Clarity also protects the guest. It reduces unexpected variation. It prevents mismatched expectations. It turns the experience into something predictable across channels, locations, dayparts, and staff. It helps teams avoid eliminating the magic of a brand in an effort to save money or shift direction. When a guest walks into a location in Ohio, they feel the exact same brand they felt in Florida. When they order on the app, the tone matches the person at the counter.

Predictability is the lifeblood of trust. Trust is the lifeblood of repeat behavior.

Without clarity, the entire organization builds in random directions. Marketing builds a tower. Tech builds a bunker. Operations builds a factory. Finance builds a fortress.

With clarity, the entire organization builds in one direction. That directional convergence creates momentum. Momentum is the most valuable asset a scaling restaurant brand can possess. It allows the brand to move faster than competitors because it spends zero energy fighting itself.

Clarity does not just guide decisions. It eliminates thousands of decisions that never should have been debated in the first place. That is its power.

Why Clarity Beats Creativity and Shortcuts

Creativity holds immense value. Shortcuts offer tempting relief. Both become dangerous liabilities when they override clarity. Creativity turns into a distraction when it demands attention during moments that require speed. Shortcuts mutate into destruction when they patch over deeper problems that clarity would have solved correctly.

Restaurant brands fall into these traps constantly alongside their agency and technology partners.

A marketing team falls in love with a creative direction that looks stunning in a slide deck. The visuals pop. The narrative flows. The concept wins awards in the boardroom yet fails to move the needle in the market. They become enamored with bells and whistles in user interface design until the system collapses under the weight of real-world usability. Marketing leaders demand flourishes to the interface that inevitably slow down ordering. The campaign prioritizes lifestyle imagery over the food itself. Creativity drifts into self-expression instead of guest-centric communication. Guests press the mental mute button and focus elsewhere when they encounter this mismatch. The brand leadership assumes the creative lacked boldness. The real issue lay in a lack of clarity.

A technology team chooses an out-of-the-box system because it checks the boxes on a requirements list. The demo looks slick. The feature set seems rich. The vendor promises the future. The system fails to reflect the brand's purpose. It ignores the workflow. It disrupts kitchen sequencing. It breaks the menu architecture. It complicates pickup needs. The software pays lip service to the brand's visual identity with a logo placement and hex codes while destroying the brand's operational soul. It introduces friction that defies remedy. It requires workarounds that the partner never addresses. It creates operational and technological debt. Leadership blames the platform. The real issue remains a lack of clarity.

Clarity reduces the surface area where bad decisions hide. It removes the impulse to over-design. It protects the guest from unnecessary choices. It stops teams from building for vanity and focuses them on building for behavior. Clarity forces a brand to accept the truth every great restaurant accepts. The experience fails if it does not work under pressure.

I had the pleasure of leading the Zaxby's account for an agency in 2016. We won the digital side of the business. Our mandate involved pulling the brand out of their circa 2005 digital experience and into the modern era with fully integrated ordering, loyalty, and location management. I got a glimpse of a shift in creative strategy for the above the line work while leading that endeavor.

Above the line refers to television, out of home, and overall campaign leadership. Agencies fight for this work. It represents the glamour of the industry.

Leadership at the time opted for a lifestyle approach. They wanted to show the product as part of the events and lives of the people. They filmed scenes of rock concerts, picnics, family gatherings, and skateboarding. Rock and roll music played while neon signs flared. The fun involved with the Zaxby's product sat in the background of the world of the people.

The strategy failed. Franchisees revolted. They wanted to see the B-level actors that the brand had used historically. They wanted the kitsch and goofiness that had defined the advertising in the past. They knew they sold chicken rather than lifestyle. They felt the creative team had lost the fun.

Zaxby's pivoted less than a year later. A goofy cowboy rode a huge buffalo chicken nugget across a prairie. Franchisees were happier. The brand went back to focusing on the food and the fun rather than a generic lifestyle.

Brands believe wild creativity will differentiate them. Clarity differentiates more powerfully. Creativity without clarity creates noise. Clarity without creativity remains strategic. The goal is to place creativity in the right part of the journey in a way that remains relevant and clear rather than removing it entirely. Creativity belongs upstream. Clarity belongs everywhere. It belongs especially at the point of action.

Jaguar provides a brutal example of poor clarity and excessive creativity outside the restaurant industry. The well-known but flailing car manufacturer launched a campaign in 2024 that baffled the market. Bright pinks flooded the screen. Androgynous actors looked as if they fell off a runway for a high-concept fashion show.

The advertisement featured quippy headlines meant to provoke. Copy Nothing and Delete Ordinary adorned the screen while models in vibrant futuristic garb marched with sledgehammers. A new Jaguar logo appeared when the chaos subsided. It represented a notable shift from the performance luxury vehicle brand enthusiasts had known. It failed to represent an actual vehicle.

The Jaguar ad lacked a car. It lacked a wheel. It featured weird models stomping around a pink background with ethereal words. The company finally released the prototype and it looked like a Dodge Magnum. The brand failed to copy nothing. They failed to delete ordinary.

The numbers confirm the disaster. The European Automobile Manufacturers Association reported forty-nine units sold in April across an entire continent. The same month saw nearly two thousand sales the year prior. That collapse reads like a brand slipping out of the conversation entirely. The year to date numbers keep the pressure on. Sales dropped seventy-five percent from January through April.

This happened because the campaign lacked clarity. It lacked alignment with the brand's offering. It opted for platitudes and ethereal statements that failed to connect with what people wanted. They bought weird when they thought they were buying cool. They actually bought confusion.

Shortcuts pose an even greater threat to clarity than bad creative. Shortcuts masquerade as efficiency. They promise speed. They promise ease. Shortcuts create tech debt and UX debt. They drive operational inconsistency and brand drift. They increase long-term cost. Shortcuts act as the counterfeit version of clarity. They present as quick wins that become lifelong problems.

Clarity slows the impulse to patch. It forces brands to address the root cause rather than the symptom. It provides the organizational backbone that shortcuts try to imitate.

Clarity functions as a survival requirement in a nonlinear world. It acts as oxygen.

Brands that prioritize clarity over creativity and shortcuts build systems that endure. They create experiences that guests trust. They build a foundation that supports the weight of the modern consumer. They stop confusing the guest and start serving them.

Clarity > Consistency > Trust > Behavior Change

Clarity acts as the foundation. Consistency builds the structure. Trust emerges as the result. Behavior change arrives as the reward. This chain represents the unbroken pattern behind every successful modern restaurant brand.

Clarity leads to consistency. Consistency leads to trust. Trust leads to predictable behavior.

Predictable behavior serves as the holy grail of restaurant economics. You cannot scale revenue without it.

Clarity creates consistency because it defines the rules that all teams follow. Each team makes local decisions without clarity. They improvise. They guess. They fill in the gaps with their own preferences. A manager in Ohio solves a problem differently than a manager in Texas. The brand fractures at the operational level. Clarity forces every team to make aligned decisions. It eliminates the gray areas where drift occurs. It reduces variation and confusion. It stops last-minute patching. Consistency becomes the natural output of a system that knows exactly what it is.

Consistency builds trust because guests crave predictability. Behavioral economics shows that people prefer a slightly inferior but predictable experience to a slightly superior but inconsistent one. This reality frustrates chefs and creatives who value novelty. But the human brain values safety. Predictability reduces cognitive load. It tells the brain that this choice is safe. It confirms that the outcome will match the expectation. Uncertainty is expensive to the brain. It burns calories. It creates anxiety. Trust reduces the risk of disappointment. In a category where disappointment is easy and alternatives are abundant, trust determines whether a brand gets considered or defaulted to.

Trust leads directly to behavior change. Trust rewires the loop. A trusted brand no longer requires exploration. It shortcuts evaluation. It becomes the option the brain selects before considering others. The guest skips the reviews. They skip the price check. They skip the debate. Trust reduces the number of competing choices to one. It creates repeatability. It decreases the need for promotions because the guest does not need a bribe to return. It increases lifetime value. It makes loyalty programs more effective because the guest actually wants to engage. It lowers acquisition cost. All because clarity built the chain.

This chain is mechanical and subliminal rather than aspirational marketing nonsense. It acts as the operating system for every brand that successfully scales past twenty-five units. The chain collapses without clarity. Trust becomes impossible without consistency. Behavior stays nonlinear without trust. Growth becomes an uphill battle of promotions and persuasion without behavior.

Consider how Jaguar could have used this chain. This speculation comes without knowledge of the inner workings of the company. But we can look at the failure through the lens of clarity.

Jaguar should have started by understanding the core needs and wants of their customer. They should have ignored the aspirational responses people give in focus groups. People lie when they want to sound sophisticated. Complaints tell the truth. Complaints point you in a better direction than desires or projected wants.

The biggest complaint by Jaguar enthusiasts over the decades was reliability. The cars were beautiful but faulty. They spent more time in the shop than on the road. Leadership should have looked at the complaints of the top competitors in the class. That research would have revealed a pattern or an open space where Jaguar could focus its evolution.

They should have dived into rebuilding a reliable luxury vehicle well-positioned against competing brands once they identified the gap. They should have done the hard thing. They should have made the investments into engineering rather than just aesthetics. They pivoted to electric vehicles as a sole offering. That was the big reveal post-ad fiasco. But they missed the step of fixing the trust issues with the brand first. They needed to invest in a niche fleet of luxury vehicles that helped people project values to the world around them. They needed to add clarity and meaning to the phrase "I drive a Jaguar."

They should have transparently told the story of the journey via social media and other exclusive channels. They should have reinforced the brand love from their most loyal and enthusiastic customer base. They ignored their base to chase a new, undefined audience. They alienated the people who kept the brand alive.

A big advertising splash should have started with an apology. "Sorry our vehicles were not up to standard. We fixed that. Here is how." Honesty drives trust better than any other tactic. An admission of fault signals confidence. It signals that the brand has corrected the issue. It closes the gap between reality and expectation.

Jaguar chose creativity over clarity. They chose a slogan like "Copy Nothing" which meant nothing. They chose imagery that confused rather than clarified. They broke the chain. They tried to skip straight to behavior change without building the consistency or trust required to earn it. The market punished them for it.

Restaurants do the same thing every day. They spend billions trying to influence behavior and build trust. But they shout at people instead of inviting them into the story. They muddy communications with lifestyle and culture rather than quality and value cues. They launch campaigns to distract from operational failures. They redesign logos to hide broken service models. They lack clarity. And clarity does more for behavior than any amount of cleverness ever could.

Clarity gives the guest a reason to trust you. Consistency gives them a reason to come back. Behavior change is simply the natural result of keeping your promises over and over again.

Stop trying to be interesting. Start trying to be clear.

Clarity Wins (and Clarity Misses) in the Real Restaurant World

Clarity is easy to admire in theory but unmistakable in practice. The restaurants that embody clarity do not do so accidentally. Their success is visible in the small decisions which are the ones most brands overlook.

Raising Cane's serves as the industry's masterclass in clarity. Their entire brand is built around one item. One. Their menu reinforces that clarity. Their operations reinforce it. Their marketing reinforces it. Their store design reinforces it. Their digital ordering reflects it. Their loyalty structure reflects it. Nothing fights the core idea. This doesn't limit the brand. It frees it and makes it frictionless.

The data proves the payoff. Raising Cane's saw systemwide sales rocket from $1.5 billion in 2020 to $3.3 billion by 2023. In the first half of 2024 alone, same-store sales jumped 17.5 percent, driven almost entirely by traffic rather than price hikes. While competitors scramble to launch complex menu innovations to capture fleeing guests, Raising Cane's founder Todd Graves has publicly stated he regrets even adding the sandwich to the menu, noting that it complicates the "One Love" focus.

Is Raising Cane's losing out on the chicken sandwich wars? Sure. One can legitimately make that argument. But adding a chicken sandwich for the sake of capitalizing on a trend that every other brand is trying to tackle isn't a strategy for growth. It's a strategy for reducing clarity and muddying the brand's magic. The brand is projected to reach $10 billion in sales by the end of the decade not by doing more, but by doing less, better.

Sweetgreen embodies clarity in a different way. Their clarity isn't about a minimal menu. It's about the emotional and functional promise of "greens, grains, and clean eating." Everything flows from that center. Their brand identity, their digital ordering flows, their seasonal menus, their pickup structures, even their app's visual hierarchy reflect one principle: uncomplicated wellness.

When Sweetgreen leans into this clarity, the results follow. Their digital revenue mix sits at a staggering 56 percent, with 30 percent coming directly through their own channels. Their "Infinite Kitchen" initiative—a fully automated makeline—isn't just a tech flex; it's an operational commitment to their core promise of speed and precision. Locations with this technology see 10 percent higher tickets and restaurant-level margins of 31 percent compared to the standard model. When they strip away the noise and focus on the engine, they win.

In-N-Out may be the strongest clarity example in U.S. restaurant history. They never expanded their menu to chase category trends. They never adopted complex LTO cycles. They never over-engineered loyalty. They never pursued vanity innovation. They built an empire on the back of radical clarity. And that clarity became legend.

That legend translates into hard loyalty metrics. In-N-Out consistently ranks number one in customer loyalty within the burger category, boasting a Net Promoter Score (NPS) of 63—miles ahead of competitors like McDonald's (19) and Burger King (-13). They don't need to buy loyalty with points because they earn it with predictability.

The misses are just as telling.

Many brands that collapsed or stalled didn't fail because of bad food. They failed because the brand never clarified what problem they were solving. They didn't take the road less traveled, the hard road, to do things a better way.

Look at Red Lobster. The brand didn't file for Chapter 11 bankruptcy in 2024 simply because people stopped eating seafood. They failed because they lost their strategic mind. The "Ultimate Endless Shrimp" promotion was a desperate, clarity-killing move that treated a premium product like a loss leader, costing the company $11 million in a single quarter. It was a promotion without purpose, a move designed to spike traffic that ultimately cannibalized the business. It was the antithesis of clarity.

Research supports this pattern of failure. Studies on menu complexity show that while variety might seem attractive, it creates "choice overload" that stalls decision-making and hurts satisfaction. Brands that cut underperforming SKUs and streamline offerings consistently see higher profitability and faster operational throughput.

Clarity is not a luxury. It is the difference between a brand that grows and a brand that spins in place.

Case Study: First Watch's 2:30pm Power Move

An empty dining room at 6:00 PM looks like a failure of imagination. Real estate is a fixed cost. Rent is due 24 hours a day. To a board of directors or a private equity firm, a dark dining room represents "idle capacity."

This is where the Funnel Fantasy usually kicks in. The logic is seductive: "We already have the kitchen. We already have the tables. Why aren't we selling burgers at night? Why aren't we capturing the dinner crowd? We are leaving millions on the table."

The pressure to "extend dayparts" is universal in the industry. It is the reason breakfast concepts launch mediocre dinner menus and dinner concepts launch confused brunch offerings. Brands chase incremental revenue, believing that "more hours" equals "more growth."

What they fail to calculate is the exponential cost of complexity. Adding dinner means adding a second shift. It means adding a second menu. It means adding shift-change chaos. It means diluting the prep focus. It means becoming "average" at two things instead of "world-class" at one.

Radical Refusal

First Watch closes at 2:30 PM. Every day. No exceptions.

While competitors scramble to add Happy Hours, late-night delivery, and extensive dinner menus to capture every possible dollar, First Watch locks the doors while the sun is still up. They have said "No" to dinner for decades. They resisted the urge to maximize utilization in favor of maximizing focus.

The "One Shift" Moat

This refusal is not a lifestyle choice; it is a strategic weapon that creates an operational moat no competitor can cross. By deleting the dinner daypart, they unlocked a level of clarity that 14-hour brands cannot compete with.

The Talent Advantage: The restaurant industry faces a chronic labor crisis. Burnout is the norm. By offering a "No Nights" schedule, First Watch attracts the best General Managers and servers in the industry—the parents who want to see their kids at night, the professionals who want a career without the grind. They don't scrape the bottom of the labor pool; they skim the top.

The Continuity of Excellence: There is no "B-Team." There is no messy handoff between the morning prep crew and the evening line. The team that opens the store is the team that closes the store. The energy remains consistent from the first egg cracked to the last check dropped.

Inventory Velocity: There are no "dinner only" SKUs dying in the walk-in cooler. There is no cross-contamination of prep lists. The menu is singular. This allows for rapid inventory turnover, which means the "Fresh" in their name is a logistical reality, not just a marketing claim.

Growth Through Subtraction

By rejecting volume, they captured value. First Watch consistently outperforms the casual dining category in traffic and same-store sales growth. They generate more revenue in 7.5 hours than many competitors generate in 15.

They proved that "idle capacity" is a myth if the active capacity is performing at an elite level.

Takeaway

Clarity is defined by what you refuse to do.

Most brands die of indigestion, not starvation. They try to be everything to everyone and end up being nothing to anyone. First Watch proved that the most profitable word in strategy is "No." When you remove the option to drift, you force the organization to dominate the one thing that remains.

CHAPTER 07
Alignment: Marketing, Tech, Finance & Operations as One System

With unity comes success; internally, externally and everywhere in between

Guests Ignore Your Org Chart

The greatest operational threat to a restaurant brand is not food cost. It's not labor shortages. It is not the saturation of the market or the rise of delivery apps. The real threat is the structural reality that most restaurant brands operate as four separate companies. Marketing runs one version. Technology runs another. Operations runs a third. Finance runs a fourth. The guest experiences the collision of all four at once.

We called this fragmentation in earlier chapters. We need to go deeper now. This looks like a people problem on the surface. It is actually a collaboration problem. The quality of collaboration determines the quality of the experience. Most multi-unit restaurant brands punish collaboration rather than foster it.

Brands historically structured themselves around channels. Marketing drove demand. Operations executed the experience. Technology kept the lights on. Finance guarded the bank account. These roles were distinct by design. The digital shift destroyed those boundaries. Technology moved from the back office to the center of the guest experience. Marketing shifted from buying ads to building ecosystems. Operations moved from execution to experience stewardship. Finance tightened the screws to ensure survival. These teams no longer handle separate responsibilities. They handle shared layers of a single system.

The modern guest ignores your internal org chart. They do not experience "marketing" separate from "operations." They experience a single chain of interactions. Influence leads to selection. Selection leads to ordering. Ordering leads to fulfillment. Fulfillment leads to satisfaction. Brands treat each stage like a different department's territory. That disconnect creates the friction that kills loyalty.

Marketing launches a limited time offer without checking operational capacity. The guest waits twenty minutes for a "fast" meal. Digital reorganizes the menu without understanding kitchen sequencing. The guest receives a cold burger. Operations changes the pickup flow without updating the app. The guest wanders the store looking for their bag. The guest never asks which department failed. They only know the brand failed.

Alignment serves as mandatory infrastructure in this era. It creates the difference between a brand that scales and a brand that stalls. It represents clarity made operational.

Thriving organizations make a fundamental shift. They stop treating marketing, tech, finance, and operations as four separate teams. They treat them as one system. They align on shared truths. They plan together. They build together. They validate together. They measure together. They launch together. They iterate together. They succeed or fail together.

This unification is required. The nonlinear guest journey demands it. An internal linear model clashes with a nonlinear guest journey. Friction is the only possible output. The guest moves fluidly from social media to search to app to store. Your teams must move just as fluidly. Fragmented teams fail to solve holistic journeys. Only a unified system can solve them.

Research supports this. Data shows that seventy percent of digital projects fail globally. The primary cause is not bad technology. It is misalignment between business objectives and project execution. When teams work in silos, they optimize for their own metrics rather than the total experience. Marketing chases clicks. Ops chases throughput. Finance chases margin. The guest chases an alternative.

Alignment means shared direction rather than blind agreement. It means shared clarity. It means shared priorities. It means shared ownership in an emotional and structural commitment to operate as a single experience organization.

I witnessed this firsthand in my role as Partner and Vice President at 3Owl. We work with the team at Mendocino Farms. I have always admired the brand. The food is delicious and clean. It makes you feel like you made the right choice. That feeling sparks other choices that build a better lifestyle.

Mendocino Farms brought something unexpected to the table when we began building their digital future. They brought true collaboration. This collaboration extended beyond our agency relationship. It permeated their internal culture. The full Mendocino Farms team shows up for every call. They remain present and attentive. They engage.

The team meets internally after our calls to align and collaborate. This spans technology and marketing into brand and beyond. The whole team stays focused and engaged. They have done this from the beginning. The result is a clear win.

The Mendocino Farms project sits three months ahead of schedule as of this writing. That is unheard of in the custom software game. We did not build things faster than expected because we are magicians. We did not bloat timelines to make ourselves look like rockstars. The client team collaborated and aligned from the start. They remained engaged. They kept communications clear.

They understand that digital transformation is not just a tech project. It is an operational project. It is a marketing project. It is a finance project. They treat it as one system.

Brands that achieve this level of alignment move faster. They waste less money. They frustrate fewer guests. They build experiences that feel seamless because the teams behind them are seamless.

The shift from four teams to one system is the only way to survive the complexity of the modern restaurant landscape. You cannot navigate a nonlinear world with a siloed map. You need a unified compass.

Alignment begins with clarity. Clarity alone fails to sustain momentum. Alignment must crystallize into shared goals, shared decisions, and shared truth for it to take hold. These three forces transform a group of disjointed departments into a unified system capable of navigating the chaos of the modern restaurant landscape.

Shared clarity serves as the anchor. It gives Marketing, Technology, Finance, and Operations the exact same definition of what the brand is and what the brand is not. Without that definition, each team builds its own interpretation. They create their own priorities. They pursue their own version of success. Marketing believes the brand is about lifestyle. Operations believes it is about speed. Finance believes it is about efficiency. Technology believes it is about innovation.

This divergence creates friction. The guest feels this friction when the app promises a customized experience that the kitchen cannot execute during a lunch rush. Shared clarity eliminates divergence. It establishes the universal rules the brand will follow. It defines the promise that every department is responsible for delivering. It ensures that the brand the guest sees on Instagram matches the brand they experience at the pickup shelf.

Clarity must convert into goals to become real. Shared goals transform alignment from theory into execution. Restaurant brands often believe they possess shared goals. They list revenue growth, smoother operations, and brand consistency on their quarterly objectives. These remain high-level aspirations rather than functional targets. Goals cannot be reached if the metrics driving them compete with one another.

Consider the standard conflict found in almost every multi-unit chain. Marketing is measured on campaign lift or social reach. Technology is measured on uptime or ticket closure. Operations is measured on speed of service or labor efficiency. Finance is measured on margin. Each team technically performs well according to their specific dashboard. Success in one area often creates stress in another.

Chapter 07: Alignment: Marketing, Tech, Finance & Operations as One System

A marketing promotion that drives demand overwhelms operations. Ticket times explode. Guest satisfaction plummets. Marketing celebrates the traffic spike while Operations drowns in the weeds. A tech rollout that reduces digital friction requires complex retraining for the staff. Speed of service drops during the adjustment period. Operations resents the new tool because it slowed them down. Finance demands labor cuts to protect margin. Staffing levels drop. The guest experience degrades.

This creates the "Cannibalization of Success." One department wins at the expense of the whole.

Shared goals eliminate this conflict. They redefine success collaboratively. A shared goal looks like increasing digital conversion by five percent while maintaining speed of service standards. It looks like reducing pickup time variability while improving guest satisfaction scores. It looks like decreasing ordering friction without increasing food waste.

These goals belong to the system rather than a single department. No single department can achieve them alone. No department can sabotage them accidentally without hurting their own metrics. Shared goals force Marketing to consider throughput capacity before launching a campaign. They force Technology to consider training loads before shipping a feature. They force Operations to value digital engagement as much as drive-thru speed.

Shared truth acts as the accelerant. It makes alignment sustainable. Shared truth represents the commitment to use data as the foundation for decision making. It replaces preference, ego, and assumption. Most restaurant organizations struggle here. Marketing looks at creative metrics. Digital looks at user experience analytics. Operations looks at service metrics. Finance looks at the P&L. Each team operates in its own data silo. None of them see the whole picture.

This creates a phenomenon known as "watermelon metrics." The dashboards look green on the outside, but the reality is red on the inside. Marketing sees green because engagement is up. Operations sees green because labor is low. But the guest sees a broken experience.

The guest produces one picture. They live in a single behavioral reality. Shared truth means seeing that reality together. It means combining marketing metrics, UX analytics, operational throughput data, ticket times, pickup accuracy, loyalty behavior, and guest satisfaction scores into one unified performance narrative.

It means no department can argue that the experience works unless the data across all layers confirms it.

Goodhart's Law states that when a measure becomes a target, it ceases to be a good measure. This happens constantly in siloed organizations. Operations targets low labor costs so aggressively that they understaff shifts and kill repeat business. Marketing targets impressions so aggressively that they attract customers who do not fit the profitability model. Shared truth corrects this. It forces the organization to look at the health of the system rather than the optics of a single metric.

Shared clarity aligns direction. Shared goals align ambition. Shared truth aligns decisions.

Organizations that operate with these three alignment forces behave differently. They move as a coordinated system. They cross-plan. They co-design. They co-evaluate. They anticipate friction before it happens. They deliver more consistent experiences because their decisions are anchored in unified intention.

This level of alignment improves everything downstream. User experience becomes simpler because design and tech fight for the same outcome. Operations become cleaner because the processes match the promise. Technology becomes smarter because it solves real problems rather than theoretical ones. Campaigns become more effective because they drive high-value traffic the kitchen can handle. Loyalty becomes more compelling because the rewards match the operational reality.

The entire experience becomes clearer because the internal model finally matches the external journey.

Alignment extends beyond goals or clarity. It defines how the work gets done. It changes the culture from a collection of warring tribes into a single organism focused on the guest. That shift is where the real transformation begins.

Technology Is the Brand's Central Nervous System

Technology functioned like plumbing for decades. It remained essential yet out of sight and out of mind. Organizations relegated it to a basement department that no one else really understood. That department handled hardware setups and wiring at new locations alongside email deliverability for corporate. Tech teams supposedly brought expertise to the table to evaluate systems across all departments from human resources and hiring software to digital ordering and drive-thru technology. They were viewed as mechanics rather than architects.

The landscape has shifted violently. Technology serves as the backbone of the restaurant experience today. It shapes the digital front door. It dictates the ordering flow. It governs the loyalty ecosystem and the kitchen display logic. It controls the pickup sequence and the labor model. It determines throughput and the guest expectation cycle. Technology constitutes the entire revenue engine. Technology operates as the restaurant experience itself rather than a mere enabler of it.

Most organizations continue to treat tech as a silo despite this reality. They bring tech in late. They use tech as a vendor manager. They inform tech of decisions instead of co-creating them. They assume tech can bend to fit the vision of marketing and the realities of operations without friction. This assumption creates failure. Tech lacks malleability. It is structural and opinionated. It demands constraints and sequence. It requires integration with every other part of the brand. Treating it as a downstream function guarantees misalignment.

Conway's Law dictates that systems inevitably reflect the communication structures of the organizations that build them. A fractured organization builds fractured systems. A brand that keeps technology in a silo builds a tech stack that operates in silos. This results in the "Frankenstack." This monstrosity consists of disparate tools bolted together with fragile APIs and hope. It creates data latency. It causes order failures. It frustrates guests who expect real-time accuracy.

Technology has ceased to function as a department. It has been democratized and has become a critical requirement for every department. Tech teams will still set up new locations with hardware and evaluate new systems. All departments must possess a nuanced and working knowledge of tech to stay competitive and effective. Marketing must understand data architecture to build effective campaigns. Operations must understand algorithm logic to manage throughput. Finance must understand SaaS scalability to forecast costs.

The tech-first mindset ensures tech is present at the moment decisions are made rather than leading every decision. Marketing, Ops, and Tech design reality when they design together. They build systems that match kitchen workflow. They build user experience flows that match guest behavior. They build loyalty logic that matches operational throughput. They avoid features that look good in creative decks but collapse at peak volume.

SpotlightAR found in recent studies that over eighty percent of digital and operational friction in restaurant brands stems from decisions made without early cross-functional tech involvement. This data reveals a clear truth. The brand suffers when tech is siloed. The brand flows when tech is integrated earlier.

Friction manifests in expensive ways. A marketing team might dream up a complex "Build Your Own Bundle" promotion. Without tech input, they fail to realize the POS cannot handle the modifier logic required to execute the bundle in the kitchen. The result involves cashiers punching in custom notes, cooks guessing at portion sizes, and inventory counts drifting into chaos. A tech-first mindset catches this constraint during the ideation phase. The team adjusts the promotion to fit the system or adjusts the system to fit the promotion before a single asset is created.

The tech-first mindset operates as a practical necessity rather than a philosophy.

It ensures feasibility. Ideas survive contact with reality because the constraints were understood upfront. It ensures scalability. Systems grow with the brand because they were architected for volume rather than patched together for speed. It ensures durability. The tech stack resists breaking under pressure because the foundation is sound. It ensures clarity. The guest experiences a seamless interaction because the backend logic matches the frontend promise.

This mindset prevents the Shortcut Trap. Organizations often feel the impulse to install quick fixes, bolt-on tools, or low-cost platforms that solve short-term problems while creating long-term dysfunction. A unified tech-first mindset rejects shortcuts because clarity has already defined the path. The team asks if the solution serves the guest. They ask if it serves the system. They ask if it serves the brand long-term.

Leaders must recognize that code is now as important as culinary. The database is as vital as the dining room. Technology acts as the connective tissue of the entire experience. It connects the promise to the execution. It connects the intent to the action. It connects the brand to the guest. Technology permeates everything.

The organizations that win the next decade will be the ones that stop treating technology like a utility and start treating it like the central nervous system of the brand.

How Real Restaurant Brands Operationalize Unity

Alignment serves as the quiet engine inside every restaurant brand that actually scales. People often perform a superficial version of alignment on stage with a keynote and a playlist. Leaders attempt to conjure it with a rousing speech and a fresh stack of laminated values. Real alignment is slower and heavier. It lives in the daily rhythm of how teams talk, plan, decide, and respond. It functions as a practice. It operates as a muscle. It forms a pattern. The restaurant brands that dominate their categories treat it as the backbone of their entire operation.

I have watched too many organizations try to will alignment into existence with a single workshop. They bring everyone into a room. They slap sticky notes on walls. They take photos to prove it happened. They leave feeling inspired. They return to their silos and slip right back into business as usual the moment the first crisis hits. The rhythm collapses because the team never actually built it. Alignment works only when it becomes a habit that shows up in every workflow, every handoff, every decision, and every launch. It works only when the brand treats alignment like a requirement instead of a luxury.

The brands that execute with precision build alignment into the structure of their business. They create rituals that force collaboration across disciplines. They remove departmental ownership from the parts of the experience that shape the guest's belief. They replace those walls with shared ownership. They make sure no one team can run ahead or lag behind. Everyone moves together. That discipline separates amateur brands from the organizations built to outlast trends and market swings.

The habit starts with experience planning. This differs entirely from campaign planning or operational roadmapping. Experience planning requires Marketing, Operations, Technology, Design, Finance, and Real Estate to sit in the same room at the top of every quarter. They lay out the next ninety days and define what the guest experience needs to deliver. They focus on the experience rather than the internal outputs. They look at every upcoming effort through that lens. Limited Time Offers (LTOs). Loyalty pushes. Digital updates. New prototype build outs. Market entries. Training cycles. Everything gets scrutinized. They ask what the experience must accomplish emotionally, operationally, behaviorally, and financially. That clarity becomes the anchor for the entire quarter.

The teams move into co-creation once intention is set. Most restaurant brands fall apart here because each discipline believes it owns a specific slice of the experience. Marketing believes it owns the message. Operations believes it owns the flow. Technology believes it owns the infrastructure. Design believes it owns the environment. Real estate believes it owns the ground.

No one owns the experience in unified organizations. Everyone owns the experience. User Experience teams shape digital flows with direct input from operations. Operations pushes back with the pressure points they know will break during peak hours. Marketing shapes the emotional clarity of every touchpoint. Architecture and design translate the voice of the brand into the physical prototype. Real Estate confirms the realities of neighborhoods and guest behavior. Finance holds everyone accountable to viability. Creation becomes collective. The work becomes cohesive because the people who must execute it crafted it together.

Activation becomes the crucible where alignment proves itself. Limited Time Offers serve as organizational moments rather than marketing moments. A well executed LTO reflects unity across the entire company. Supply Chain verifies availability. Operations adjusts build processes and line choreography. Technology sets up menu logic and conversion pathways. Training equips the field with understanding and muscle memory. Marketing tells a story that feels true. Finance predicts volume and adjusts expectations. An LTO hits the market with that level of preparation and feels effortless from the outside. The entire company moved together behind the scenes to make that happen.

The same level of unity applies when brands build or evolve physical prototypes. Successful restaurants reject redesigning stores based on aesthetics alone. They rebuild the physical experience with cross-functional truth at the table. Operations validates every station design and movement pattern. Technology integrates hardware and digital ordering into the layout. Marketing ensures the environment communicates the brand's personality and promise. Real Estate grounds the concept in the realities of visibility, accessibility, and market behavior. Architecture gives the brand a shape that feels inevitable. Prototype work becomes an expression of the entire organization rather than a design team working in isolation.

Market entry becomes another arena where alignment decides whether the brand succeeds or stumbles. A unified organization refuses to drop a store into a new city and hope for the best. They study the cultural and behavioral patterns of the market. They identify the neighborhoods where their ideal guest profile thrives. They prepare operations for labor realities. They build marketing strategies that match the heartbeat of the new region. They set technology and loyalty structures to support early adoption. They test the prototype against the market's expectations. Expansion becomes a strategic maneuver shaped by every discipline instead of a rushed land grab.

Evaluation serves as the habit that keeps alignment alive. The brands that scale review performance weekly or biweekly. They look at metrics that reflect the total guest experience. They ignore vanity metrics isolated by department. They focus on experience metrics. Order accuracy. Pickup consistency. Throughput stability. Digital conversion. Loyalty engagement. Prototype performance. Campaign lift. Market penetration. Everyone sees the same numbers. Everyone responds to the same truth. No special dashboards exist to comfort specific leaders. Reality rules the room. Teams share responsibility when they share reality.

Launches become the final checkpoint. Unified brands never let a feature, promotion, prototype, or market opening go live without shared signoff. Marketing signs off on clarity. Operations signs off on execution. Technology signs off on functionality. Design signs off on cohesion. Finance signs off on viability. Shared ownership eliminates the instinct to point fingers. Success is collective. Failure is collective. That kind of accountability builds maturity in a brand.

The final ritual remains the most important one. Every decision anchors around the guest. Preference and ego take a back seat. Departmental agendas disappear. Behavioral truth guides the choices. Teams look at the Messy Middle. They analyze funnel data. They study market dynamics and demand patterns. They respect pricing sensitivity and guest psychology. Teams anchor themselves in truth because truth removes opinion from the table. Decisions become sharper and faster when the guest becomes the north star.

Alignment operates as an operating system rather than a soft skill. Everything tightens when it becomes ritual. The digital experience becomes cleaner. The physical experience becomes more intentional. Marketing becomes more precise. Operations become more resilient. Market entries land with more confidence. Guests feel the difference even if they cannot explain it. They sense that the brand moves with purpose. They trust it because it behaves like it knows who it is.

Alignment transforms strategy into action. Action transforms into momentum. Momentum serves as the force that lets a brand scale without losing itself.

The New Model

Turning the paradigm shift into an executable system for modern restaurant brands.

The diagnosis is complete. We stripped the engine down to the block. You understand why the old parts failed. You see why the funnel broke. You see why shortcuts created debt. You see why archetypes provide the necessary psychological anchor.

Knowledge alone changes nothing. Insights do not ship code. Philosophy does not serve food.

Part III marks the transition from understanding the problem to engineering the solution. We call this The New Model. It serves as the operating system for the nonlinear world.

We move from the why to the how in this section. We translate behavioral truth into digital architecture. We turn archetypal alignment into user experience design. We convert clarity into operational reality.

You cannot build a modern restaurant brand with antique tools. You need a system designed for the loop rather than the line. You need infrastructure that prioritizes confidence over persuasion. You need a way to work that forces alignment rather than hoping for it.

This is the blueprint. It is time to build.

CHAPTER 08
Designing for Real Behavior

Crafting the guest experience in the realities of today's guest journey

Experience Is the Brand, Not the Campaign

Here is how we kill the Outdated Funnel. We kill it by embracing experience as the only opportunity to win that matters.

Most restaurant brands still treat experience like an afterthought. They view it as a downstream task to be polished once the "important" work is finished. They define the brand strategy. They build the campaign. They launch the flashy Limited Time Offer. They freshen the visuals. Then—and only then—do they look at the experience. That mindset sabotages them before they even start.

The experience is not a layer of execution. The experience is the brand. Every part of it. Nothing lives above it.

A brand is not the story you tell in a boardroom or a thirty-second spot. It is the feeling you leave behind. It is the full weight of every touchpoint a guest interacts with whether you planned it or not. It is the search result that pulls them in. It is the digital flow they navigate in a rush. It is the way the kitchen communicates with the front of house. It is the reliability of the pickup shelf. It is the moment they open the bag and take the first bite. It is the consistency of the system that supports all of it. A brand does not live in ideas. A brand lives in the system that delivers the experience.

This is where the truth becomes unavoidable. You cannot build a modern restaurant brand through campaigns or color palettes or clever storytelling alone. You build it by designing the system that shapes behavior. The system becomes the brand. When that system contradicts itself or collapses under pressure, the brand breaks.

Guests do not forgive broken systems. Not when they are hungry. Not when they are busy. Not when they trusted you to make their day easier. A great ad campaign can get a guest to the door, but only a great system can bring them back. If the marketing promises magic and the operations deliver chaos, the guest registers that gap as a lie.

The Messy Middle taught us that decision making is scattered, emotional, and fluid. But what happens after the guest chooses you is just as crucial. The evaluation begins instantly. It happens below the level of language. It happens in the body before the mind catches up.

Neuroscience calls this "somatic processing." The brain constantly scans the environment for threats and friction. When a guest encounters a slow loading screen, a confusing menu board, or a disorganized pickup counter, their brain releases cortisol. They feel a micro-stress. They may not articulate it as "bad UX," but their body records it as "avoid next time." Conversely, when a flow is seamless and the food is ready exactly when promised, the brain releases dopamine. It records the experience as "safe" and "rewarding."

Did the digital flow move cleanly? Did the promise you implied show up in the reality you delivered? Did the pickup feel intuitive or confusing? Did the food hold its integrity? Did the process respect their time? The guest may not articulate these questions, but their behavior answers them with clarity.

Experience design is not a beautification exercise. It is an operational discipline. The brain is not waiting for creative expression. The brain is looking for relief. It wants ease. It wants speed. It wants a frictionless journey that asks nothing unnecessary of it.

Every second you waste, you lose belief. Every second you save, you earn it.

When you design for behavior, you stop shaping the brand solely around what you want the guest to feel. You start shaping the system around what the guest actually needs. That shift unlocks everything. It forces clarity. It forces restraint. It forces teams to prioritize usefulness over self-expression.

Brands that cling to outdated thinking learn the consequences slowly and painfully. They produce experiences that celebrate their own creativity but drain the patience of their guests. Consider the earlier example of Fresh 2 Order's traffic flow. They built for themselves instead of the people paying the bill. They imagined guests craving theatrics when guests craved things that work. They prioritized the aesthetic of the entrance over the logic of the exit.

Modern restaurant success happens when the system becomes a source of clarity at every step. You feel clarity in the flow. You feel it in the sequence. You feel it in the way the brand takes care of you without requiring thought.

Campaign-first brands burn bright but rarely sustain. They generate spikes instead of stability. They rely on the dopamine hit of novelty to drive traffic. But novelty fades. System-first brands build momentum because they remove friction from the experience. They create consistency that acts like gravity.

Behavioral science has been shouting this for decades. Daniel Kahneman's concept of "System 1" thinking explains that humans prefer fast, intuitive, automatic decisions. We avoid "System 2" thinking, which is slow, deliberate, and calorie-expensive. A restaurant system that forces a guest to think—to figure out where to park, how to modify an item, or where to stand—forces them into System 2. It feels like work.

Restaurants feel this pressure more intensely than almost any other category because the guest arrives hungry. A hungry brain is an impatient brain. It is distracted. It is constrained by time. It is short on patience. A restaurant system that understands this wins without shouting.

Experience is not an accent on your brand. It is the machinery underneath. It is the part the guest touches. It is the part the guest trusts. It is the part that carries the entire weight of the brand whether you acknowledge it or not.

If you want to fix your brand, stop fixing your ads. Fix your system.

The Experience Chain: Exploration > Evaluation > Experience

If experience acts as the brand, then the Experience Chain serves as the structure the brand depends on. Restaurants often talk about the "guest journey," but the journey most brands map is a staged sequence with fictional motivations. It is a relic of a linear past. The Experience Chain is not imagined. It is observable. It represents the three-part behavioral cycle every guest moves through whether they are aware of it or not.

Exploration. Evaluation. Experience.

Exploration is the pre-choice environment. It is the place where desires are sparked, options are surfaced, and possibilities begin to form. This is where creative influence matters, but only in a controlled way. Exploration happens on TikTok, Instagram, and YouTube. It happens on Google, Maps, UberEats, DoorDash, and Yelp. It happens in the breakroom when a coworker mentions a new burger spot. It is where food becomes an idea before it becomes a choice.

Restaurants often misunderstand exploration. They think this is where they must "sell the brand." They try to close the deal before the guest is even hungry. But exploration is not persuasion. It is priming.

Byron Sharp, in his seminal work How Brands Grow, describes this as building "Mental Availability." You are not trying to force a transaction. You are trying to ensure that when the trigger of hunger strikes, your brand is one of the few that lights up in the guest's memory structures. Your presence in the exploration phase must be recognizable, clear, culturally relevant, and consistent. The job of exploration is simply to enter the guest's possibility set.

The data shifts how we must view this phase. Google Senior Vice President Prabhakar Raghavan famously admitted that nearly 40 percent of young people, when looking for a place for lunch, do not go to Google Maps or Search. They go to TikTok or Instagram. They explore visually. They explore socially. If your brand is not legible in those spaces—if it does not look like something worth eating in a three-second video loop—you do not even enter the chain.

Evaluation is where that possibility set narrows. It is where guests compare choices based on heuristics. They scan for proximity, speed, price, reviews, past experience, value, and predictability. Evaluation is where brand promises get judged before they are experienced. This is where Google's Messy Middle loops live. This is where BCG's influence map activates.

Evaluation is the filter. It is the moment the brain switches from "What could I eat?" to "What should I eat?"

This phase is governed by risk reduction. The brain is risk-averse, especially when hungry. Guests use social proof as a proxy for safety. A Harvard Business School study found that a one-star increase in Yelp rating leads to a 5-9 percent increase in revenue. Why? Not because the food suddenly tastes better, but because the risk of a bad experience dropped in the guest's mind.

Evaluation is not where you "win the guest's heart." It is where you either reduce uncertainty or increase it. Reduce uncertainty and you move to the final stage. Increase it and you are eliminated.

This is why clarity in digital channels is lethal to competitors. If Brand A displays a clear wait time, a legible menu, and a straightforward price, and Brand B forces the user to download a PDF menu or call for details, Brand A wins. Not because they are better, but because they are easier to evaluate.

Experience is the moment after the decision. It is the fulfillment of the promise. It is the digital ordering flow, the pickup process, the packaging integrity, the operational execution, the food, the speed, and the ease. This is where trust is either built or destroyed.

Psychology offers us the "Peak-End Rule" here. Nobel laureate Daniel Kahneman discovered that people judge an experience largely based on how they felt at its peak (the most intense point) and at its end, rather than based on the total sum or average of every moment of the experience.

For a restaurant, the "Peak" is usually the first bite of food. The "End" is the pickup or payment process. If the food is delicious (High Peak) but the pickup was chaotic and stressful (Low End), the guest remembers the chaos more vividly than the flavor. The chain breaks.

Experience is not just operations. It is the emotional residue of the system.

Here lies the part most brands miss. Experience is not the end of the chain. Experience becomes the beginning of the next exploration moment.

Experience is the input that feeds future choices.

When the chain works correctly, experience transitions into habit. If the experience was positive, predictable, and frictionless, the brain records it as a "solved problem." The next time the guest is hungry, they skip the Evaluation phase entirely. They do not compare you. They do not read reviews. They do not check prices. They default to you.

This is the Loyalty Loop. McKinsey & Company identified that post-purchase experience is the primary driver of the next purchase cycle. If exploration earns attention and evaluation earns confidence, experience earns behavior.

This is why brands must treat the Experience Chain as their operating model. Every interaction must reinforce the chain:

Exploration: Make it recognizable and interesting. Be mentally available where the guest is looking.

Evaluation: Make it predictable and trustworthy. Remove every ounce of friction and ambiguity.

Experience: Make it effortless and preferable. Deliver on the Peak and protect the End.

When even one part of the chain fails, the next chain weakens. A great ad (Exploration) leads to a confusing menu (Evaluation), causing the guest to bail. A seamless order (Evaluation) leads to a cold meal (Experience), ensuring they never return.

When all three align, the chain compounds. The guest moves through it faster each time. Eventually, the chain becomes a circle. The guest stops exploring and starts repeating.

This compounding effect separates brands that scale from brands that stall. Chains are not built by accident. They are built by design. And design demands behavioral logic—not aesthetic preference.

Three Layers of One Behavioral Engine

When you understand the Experience Chain, you understand why marketing, technology, and operations must function as one. You realize that the traditional silos are not just inefficient; they are destructive. UX, CX, and Ops are not separate disciplines. They are three expressions of the same behavioral engine.

UX: The Communication Layer. CX: The Delivery Layer. Ops: The Execution Layer.

These three layers determine whether the Experience Chain works or collapses. UX sets expectations. CX confirms them. Ops fulfills them. When these layers contradict one another, the guest feels the seam immediately. When they reinforce one another, the guest feels clarity.

UX (User Experience) is often misunderstood by restaurant leadership as "app design" or "making things look pretty." This is a fatal simplification. UX is not about prettiness or clever creativity. UX is cognitive alignment.

It is the way you communicate with the guest through digital surfaces, signage, menu architecture, ordering flows, labels, and instructions. Good UX feels invisible. It feels fast, legible, and respectful. It reduces decisions rather than creating them. It eliminates the need for explanation.

UX acts as the interface between the guest's intent and the brand's capability. If the UX allows a guest to order a complex modification that the kitchen cannot execute during peak hours, the UX has failed. It wrote a check the operations team could not cash.

Hick's Law states that the time it takes to make a decision increases with the number and complexity of choices. Bad UX ignores this. It bombards the guest with upsells, pop-ups, and unclear categories. This causes "decision fatigue." When UX fails, guests hesitate. Hesitation is friction. Friction increases abandonment.

CX (Customer Experience) is the holistic reality. It is the delivery layer. It represents the consistency of the experience from the guest's perspective as they traverse from digital to physical and back again.

CX is the credibility of your promises. It is whether the pickup estimate matches reality. It is whether the packaging protects the temperature of the food. It is whether the line moves at the speed your systems implied. It is whether loyalty redemptions feel easy or burdensome. CX is the embodiment of your brand's integrity.

Forrester Research defines CX quality across three dimensions: effectiveness (value), ease (usability), and emotion (how the interaction made the customer feel). In a restaurant, CX is the bridge. If UX is the map, CX is the terrain. You can draw a straight line on a map (UX), but if the terrain is a swamp (bad CX), the map is useless.

Ops (Operations) is the beating heart. It is the execution layer. It is the physics of the brand.

Ops is the choreography behind the scenes that determines whether the promise and reality align. It is the sequencing of the kitchen. It is the clarity of prep. It is the accuracy of timing. It is the reliability of labor. It is the predictability of execution. Ops is where the brand becomes physical.

If Ops fails, CX fails immediately. If CX fails, UX functions as a broken promise. The best app in the world cannot save a cold burger. The most beautiful digital menu cannot fix a rude interaction at the counter.

The Danger of Disconnection

When these three layers are designed separately, they contradict one another. This happens in almost every scaling chain.

The Marketing/UX team designs a "Build Your Own" interface with infinite customization options because they think it drives engagement. They deploy it.

The Ops team realizes that these infinite modifications slow down the make-line by 15 seconds per order. Throughput crashes. The CX result is a lobby full of angry people waiting for food that is late and potentially wrong.

The UX promised freedom. The Ops delivered chaos. The CX delivered disappointment.

Guests feel this inconsistency. Inconsistency destroys trust.

The Power of Synchronization

The system becomes cohesive when these layers are designed together.

UX sets the correct expectations because it understands Ops. A smart UX team knows the kitchen's capacity. They design the digital menu to match the station layout of the kitchen. They use "throttling" logic to remove items from the app when the kitchen is overwhelmed. They guide the guest toward items that are easy to execute during rush hours.

Ops executes correctly because it understands UX. The kitchen display system (KDS) is designed to match the flow of the order as the guest entered it. The terminology used in the back of house matches the terminology used in the app. The packaging is designed to hold the specific items promoted in the digital channel.

CX becomes seamless because it understands both. The quote time algorithm (CX) reads the kitchen load (Ops) and updates the app (UX) in real-time. The guest is told "20 minutes" and the food is ready in 19.

Behavioral economists call this Expectation Confirmation Theory. Satisfaction is a function of expectation minus reality.

If Expectation (UX) is high and Reality (Ops) is low, Satisfaction is negative.

If Expectation (UX) is managed accurately and Reality (Ops) meets it, Satisfaction is positive.

Domino's Pizza provides the gold standard case study for this unification. Their "Pizza Tracker" is not just a marketing gimmick. It is a masterpiece of UX, CX, and Ops integration.

UX: The tracker reduces anxiety by showing progress. It creates transparency.

Ops: The data comes from sensors and inputs in the actual kitchen. It forces the line to be disciplined.

CX: The promise (hot pizza) matches the reality (delivery at the door).

Domino's didn't just build a tracker. They built a feedback loop where the digital layer enforces the operational layer.

The Unified Mechanism

UX, CX, and Ops are three layers of one mechanism: Trust.

Every time the UX makes a claim, the Ops must prove it true. Every time Ops executes, CX scores the win.

The systems that scale in the modern restaurant world are the ones where UX, CX, and Ops speak the same language. They follow the same rules. They honor the same clarity. These brands do not create "experiences" in the abstract sense. They create systems that produce experience. They do it repeatably. They do it reliably. They do it predictably.

When you align these three layers, you stop managing chaos and start managing momentum.

Designing Systems the Brain Loves

Every positive restaurant experience is built on four psychological forces that sit deep inside the human brain. Clarity. Speed. Predictability. Satisfaction. These forces are not poetic ideas. They are measurable behavioral realities that shape how people choose, judge, and return to a restaurant. They determine whether a guest feels cared for or punished. They determine whether the brand becomes a habit or a memory. They determine whether the business grows or grinds.

Clarity lowers cognitive strain. Speed lowers emotional tension. Predictability lowers uncertainty. Satisfaction lowers resistance to returning. When these four forces line up, the guest forms trust. Trust becomes pattern. Pattern becomes frequency. Frequency becomes the engine that keeps the brand alive.

The work begins with clarity. The human brain is constantly burning energy to make decisions. Every step you ask a guest to take drains a little more of that energy. Clarity gives some of that energy back. Clarity makes the next step obvious. Clarity removes doubt. The simplest examples say everything. A menu that shows people where to look before they start squinting. A digital flow that leads the eye through a clean sequence. A pickup process that makes the guest feel confident instead of awkward. A value equation that explains itself without a single extra word. Clarity is not minimalism. It is guidance. The kind of guidance the brain craves without ever admitting it.

When clarity disappears, the guest begins to work. They decode. They interpret. They search. They hesitate. They second guess. That extra effort becomes mental drag. Mental drag becomes frustration. Frustration pushes them toward a different brand on their next visit because the brain always remembers the places where it had to work too hard. Clarity removes all of that friction before it can start.

Speed is the next behavioral force. Speed is not the speed of production schedules or creative turnarounds. Speed is the removal of unnecessary steps. Fewer taps. Fewer modifiers. Fewer decisions. Cleaner logic. Faster reinforcement cues. A digital flow that moves without hesitation. A drive thru lane that feels like momentum instead of waiting. A handoff that happens at the exact moment the guest expects it. Speed reduces emotional friction. It lowers the stress that builds inside the guest when they are hungry, tired, distracted, or running between obligations. Most restaurant guests arrive in that state. Speed is not an advantage. It is a lifeline that protects their intent.

The next force is predictability. Predictability comes from consistency. Consistent flows. Consistent packaging. Consistent quality. Consistent pickup cues. Consistent timing. Consistent communication. Predictability settles the mind. It lowers uncertainty. It removes the need for the brain to scan for threats or surprises. Predictability creates the sense of safety that lets a guest choose the same brand again without hesitation.

Predictability also quiets the Messy Middle. When the brain is overwhelmed with options, it looks for familiarity. It looks for the choice that feels safe. It looks for the place where it knows exactly what will happen. Predictability gives the brain an anchor. The anchor holds even when competitors are louder, flashier, or more inventive. The brain chooses the known system because effort is the enemy. Predictability guarantees a familiar path that protects the guest from cognitive overload.

Satisfaction is the final force and the one that ties the entire system together. Satisfaction does not come from delight. Delight is too unreliable. Satisfaction comes from coherence. Coherence is the feeling that every part of the experience came from the same truth. The digital flow matched the operational reality. The pickup process matched the communication pattern. The food quality matched the promise. Nothing felt out of place. Nothing felt improvisational. Nothing felt like the brand was guessing. Coherence gives the guest the emotional exhale that tells them they made the right choice.

Satisfaction strengthens the memory of the visit. Memory strengthens the likelihood of return. Return strengthens frequency. Frequency strengthens the economics of the business. Guests do not articulate this process. They simply feel it. Their behavior tells the story.

Brands that master these four drivers never chase gimmicks. They do not rely on stunts or bursts of creativity. They do not need oversized promotions to carry them. Their experience becomes their marketing. Their clarity becomes their value. Their system becomes their differentiator. Guests become the advocates because the brand behaves with consistency and confidence.

The truth is simple. When a restaurant designs for real human behavior, it stops wrestling for loyalty. Loyalty emerges on its own because the brand did the work that makes people return without effort. Loyalty stops being a program. It becomes a natural response to a reliable system.

This is the work that gives every other part of the brand its power. Clarity strengthens the first moment. Speed strengthens the journey. Predictability strengthens the expectation. Satisfaction strengthens the memory. Together, they build the kind of experience that becomes instinctive. Guests choose the brand without thinking because the brand has earned that reflex.

When a restaurant earns loyalty through behavior, the business finally feels lighter. Every decision becomes easier. Every campaign performs better. Every new product fits more cleanly. Every new location opens with more confidence. The brand grows because the system is doing the heavy lifting.

This is the foundation. The next section breaks into the structure of that foundation and reveals the chains that hold the entire experience together.

Key Takeaways: What Leaders Must Know Now

1. Experience is the brand.

Campaigns, LTOs, visuals, and messaging do not build modern restaurant brands. Systems do. The guest only trusts what the system delivers, not what the brand claims. When the system breaks, the brand breaks.

2. Behavior, not creativity, defines the success of the experience.

The brain is not waiting to be entertained. It is waiting to be relieved. Clarity, speed, predictability, and satisfaction shape guest behavior far more powerfully than aesthetics or storytelling.

3. The Experience Chain is the real operating model.

Exploration → Evaluation → Experience is the actual sequence guests move through. Not the funnel. Not the imaginary journeys in brand decks. The chain is observable, measurable, and unforgiving when misaligned.

4. Exploration is priming, not persuasion.

In early stages, the job is to enter the consideration set—not force a decision. Recognition and relevance matter more than being loud or clever.

5. Evaluation is uncertainty reduction.

Guests choose brands that minimize risk, not brands with the flashiest promotions. Social proof, convenience, clarity, and credibility drive selection.

6. Experience is the decisive moment—and the beginning of the next cycle.

The real evaluation happens after the choice. Experience determines whether exploration next time starts with your brand or someone else's. Experience earns habit.

7. UX, CX, and Ops are one behavioral engine—not three departments.

UX sets expectations. CX verifies them. Ops fulfills them. If any layer contradicts the others, trust collapses instantly. Integrated design is not optional; it is the only viable model.

8. System-first beats-campaign first every time.

Campaign-first brands spike. System-first brands sustain. Guests return to brands that minimize effort, not brands that yell the loudest.

9. The four psychological forces determine loyalty.

Clarity reduces cognitive strain.

Speed reduces emotional tension.

Predictability reduces uncertainty.

Satisfaction reduces hesitation to return.

Master these and loyalty emerges naturally.

10. Behavioral design reduces the cost of growth.

When the system does the heavy lifting, every campaign improves, every initiative integrates more cleanly, and every new location opens with less drag. The system becomes the engine of scale.

Action Items: What Leaders Must Do Now

1. Rebuild the brand definition around experience, not messaging.

Stop treating the experience as a downstream "execution layer." Rewrite what the brand stands for in terms of the behaviors and systems that support it.

Ask: What do we want guests to do, and what system would make that behavior effortless?

2. Map your true Experience Chain.

Audit real guest behavior across Exploration, Evaluation, and Experience. Identify friction points, broken promises, unclear expectations, and mismatched cues.

Deliverable: A three-part diagnostic showing where the chain strengthens or collapses.

3. Replace department KPIs with Experience Chain KPIs.

Shift from campaign metrics to clarity, flow, friction, reliability, and satisfaction metrics tied to real behavior.

Ask: What does the guest feel here? What does the data show they actually did?

4. Conduct an expectation-matching review across UX, CX, and Ops.

Ensure digital language, operational sequencing, and in-person experience tell one coherent story.

Deliverable: A list of mismatches between what UX implies and what Ops delivers.

5. Implement a behavioral design checklist for all new initiatives.

Before approving anything—new flows, packaging, menu changes, pickup processes—require a review against the four forces: clarity, speed, predictability, satisfaction.

Question: Where does this create friction? Where does it create relief?

6. Redesign digital surfaces for cognitive ease, not creativity.

Simplify ordering flows, reduce taps, eliminate ambiguity, make pickup instructions explicit.

Goal: Reduce cognitive load by 30 percent across the digital journey.

7. Strengthen operational choreography to support the promise.

If Ops cannot deliver what UX says, UX is lying. Re-choreograph prep-lines, pickup shelves, packaging, and staffing models to support the system.

Outcome: Predictable throughput that matches communicated expectations.

8. Clarify the value equation at every touchpoint.

Guests should instantly understand what they're getting, why it matters, and why it's worth it.

Task: Rewrite value messaging for simplicity and precision.

9. Build a cross-functional Experience Council.

Marketing, Digital, Ops, Finance, and Culinary meet weekly to review the Experience Chain, address friction, and align initiatives.

Outcome: Prevent misalignment before it hits the guest.

10. Make the system the hero internally.

Stop praising departments for independent accomplishments. Praise integrated wins that reduce friction, increase speed, improve predictability, or elevate satisfaction.

Shift: From celebrating noise to celebrating coherence.

CHAPTER 09
Data-Backed Decision Making

Repositioning tech as the new foundation for brand success

People Lie, Data Doesn't

Data has become the most misunderstood force in the modern restaurant world. Leaders love to proclaim they are "data-driven," but in practice, they remain emotion-driven with data sitting in the passenger seat holding a map no one actually follows.

Restaurants have always functioned as emotional organisms. They were built on instinct. They were built on taste. They were built on hospitality, hustle, and the courage to trust a gut feeling. Those instincts built legendary brands long before digital funnels and attribution models existed. But those instincts no longer scale on their own.

The guest journey is too messy. The platforms are too fast. The touchpoints are too numerous. The patterns are too nonlinear. No leader can watch the full experience from the dining room corner anymore. Data has become the only mirror strong enough to reveal the truth.

And that truth kills the Bias Loop.

The Bias Loop whispers to leaders that their instincts are correct. It nudges teams into confirming what they already believe. It twists data into validation instead of revelation. It turns research into a weapon that protects the plan instead of improving it. The Bias Loop hides inside analysis because analysis feels rigorous even when it is simply reinforcing the decision leaders already want to make.

Ronald Coase, the Nobel Prize-winning economist, famously said, "If you torture the data long enough, it will confess to anything." Nowhere does the Bias Loop thrive more than in this torture chamber. It is the breeding ground where opinion dresses itself up as evidence. Teams pull the numbers that support their position and ignore the ones that challenge it. They present dashboards that tell the story they want to tell. They cherry-pick metrics that flatter performance. They claim the data proves their point when all it proves is their preference. That is not analysis. That is a story told with numbers.

Remember the Cracker Barrel example from Chapter 2? That wasn't just bias; it was a failure to distinguish Stated Preference from Revealed Preference. The data wasn't wrong; the interpretation was. The leadership team likely looked for data to validate a modernization strategy rather than looking for data that revealed the emotional anchor of the brand. The Bias Loop shaped the story before the story ever reached the brand.

This is the risk every restaurant faces today. Data does not save organizations from bias. It amplifies the impact of bias when used incorrectly. When brands view data as validation, they weaponize it against reality. When brands view data as confrontation, they strengthen themselves.

Data is meant to challenge the plan, not protect it.

Data is not a spreadsheet. It is a behavioral mirror. It shows what guests actually do even when those behaviors contradict what leaders believe. It reveals whether the digital funnel carried people or lost them. It exposes operational drift. It shows where pickup timing sinks under pressure. It reveals whether loyalty drives true incremental value or just shifts the calendar. It shows the truth of the Invisible Journey between intention and completion. A truth no one can guess. A truth no leader can intuit.

Restaurant organizations now sit on more behavioral data than at any point in history.

Digital Flows: Where does the thumb stop scrolling? Where does the cart get abandoned?

Search Behavior: What keywords are guests using before they find you?

Kitchen Pacing: How long does a ticket sit on the KDS before the first bump?

Loyalty Triggers: Do points actually change frequency, or are you just discounting your regulars?

Inventory Correlations: Does a specific menu modification correlate with higher food waste?

Sentiment Diffusion: What is the mood in the reviews, not just the star rating?

These signals do not just show what happened. They show why it happened. They highlight the tension inside the system. They reveal where the brand's promises snap under real-world conditions.

But the data only becomes transformative when it replaces assumptions instead of supporting them. Most brands do the opposite. They use data as a justification engine. They find the metrics that validate the decisions they already made. They interpret noise as proof. They limit analysis to numbers that flatter. That practice does not create clarity. It creates delusion. And delusion kills brands quietly.

Data is confrontation.

A spike in bounce rate might look like a messaging issue to marketing. Data confronts that opinion: heatmaps show guests never found the "Order Now" button because the hero image pushed it below the fold.

A new operational process might feel smoother to the field operations team. Data confronts that feeling: the KDS logs show that while the front line is happier, the kitchen makes times increased by forty seconds per ticket.

A platform rollout might feel like progress to the tech team because the code is clean. Data confronts that pride: session recordings show that the ordering flow grew two steps longer, causing a 15% drop in conversion.

A loyalty promo might look successful to leadership because revenue spiked on Tuesday. Data confronts that celebration: cohort analysis shows those guests simply shifted their Friday visit to Tuesday to get the deal, resulting in zero net incremental revenue.

This is the difference between brands that evolve and brands that erode. Brands that evolve let data challenge them. Brands that erode let data flatter them.

In a guest-centered system, data becomes the great equalizer. It removes the power of opinion. It stops the loudest voice in the room from hijacking the experience. It creates a single source of truth that every team must follow. And that truth forces the organization to respond to reality instead of preference. It eliminates the ego from decision-making. It eliminates the political layering that slows momentum. It eliminates the internal storytelling that convinces teams everything is fine when everything is actually drifting.

The best restaurant brands treat data like oxygen. Not a resource. A requirement. They breathe it. They move with it. They build on it. They let it shape their choices instead of their narratives. They let it expose weak points. They let it humble them. They let it strengthen them.

Data becomes truth when the organization accepts that truth matters more than ego. Data becomes power when every department works from the same truth. Data becomes transformation when that truth forces the system to change.

How Data Exposes Friction

Friction is the true rival in today's restaurant industry. It is not the brand next door doing a louder campaign. It is the invisible drag inside your own operation.

Quiet Killers

Most restaurants do not lose guests because the food stinks. They rarely lose guests because a competitor simply has a better slogan. They lose guests because the experience accumulates micro-breaks. Friction creeps in quietly. It leaves quietly. No complaint reaches the inbox to warn you. No angry tweet goes viral. The guest simply does not come back.

The silent exit is the deadliest metric in the business. Research from PwC indicates that thirty-two percent of all customers would stop doing business with a brand they loved after just one bad experience. In the high-velocity, low-loyalty world of restaurants, that number is likely higher.

This is why data serves as the only reliable way to expose this invisible enemy. Guests do not log formal complaints stating, "I was annoyed by the pickup shelf configuration" or "the ordering screen made me pause for five seconds." They just abandon. They change brands. They grow silent. Their absence is the message.

But you only hear that message if you are watching. You only see it if your systems are listening.

Data shows you the drop-off points. It reveals the silent exits. It tracks the latent behavior shifts. Until you dig into the analytics, you will continue to believe guests return because they liked your food. You are wrong. They return because the system didn't make them think. They didn't over-wait. They didn't feel the drag.

Friction lives in the invisible seams of a restaurant journey. It shows up in places you might not suspect, yet the data captures every stumble:

The Homepage Freeze: A menu overloaded with options leaves the decision frozen. Data reveals a high bounce rate on the menu page with low scroll depth. The guest arrived, got overwhelmed, and left.

The Load Time Tax: A menu category takes too long to load on a mobile device. Google research shows that fifty-three percent of visits are abandoned if a mobile site takes longer than three seconds to load. Data reveals this as a sharp drop-off between "Menu View" and "Add to Cart."

The Modifier Maze: A modifier screen is so cluttered guests pause and second-guess. Session recordings show "rage clicks" or long pauses followed by cart abandonment.

The Checkout Ambush: A checkout screen reveals surprise fees and forces hesitation. Data shows a high rate of "Cart Abandonment" at the final step, signaling a breach of trust.

The Phantom Pickup: A pickup window changes location mid-order without notice. Operational data shows a spike in "Guest Arrival to Order Handout" time, indicating confusion in the lobby.

The Quote Time Lie: An order quote time feels unrealistic and triggers doubt. Data comparing "Promised Time" vs. "Actual Handout Time" reveals a gap that destroys trust.

The Interruption: A loyalty prompt is inserted before the menu appears. Data shows a drop in conversion immediately following the popup.

Each one of those moments has a behavioral signature. Each one is measurable.

Analytics reveal the hotspots: digital abandonment rates, scroll-depth drop-offs, session heatmaps, and lag spikes. Operational dashboards show disparities: ticket time variability, order accuracy dips, and Kitchen Display System (KDS) bottlenecks. Loyalty records show break-points: redemption drop-off and months of silence after a single promo. Discovery data shows fewer clicks, decreased proximity conversions, and softening map engagement.

In a world built on behavior, these are the signals of friction. The patterns make the invisible visible.

The key detail to remember is that friction is not random. Friction is patterned. It happens where the internal model of your brand contradicts the behavioral model of the guest.

Marketing throws in a hero image and a lengthy promotion before Tech and Operations signed off. Tech delivers a rollout without consulting Operations on peak volume flows. Operations cheats a queue layout change without notifying digital ordering. One misalignment, one moment of mis-sequenced experience, and the entire journey stutters.

That stutter costs belief.

Research backs this up. A study in the Journal of Travel & Tourism Marketing found that service-failure severity in dining experiences correlates directly to switching intention. Guests don't simply complain; they shift. Industry briefs show that reducing friction is directly tied to higher throughput and guest satisfaction in restaurant contexts. When you view these metrics as outcome levers, not just performance scoreboards, you stop chasing campaigns and start fixing the system.

The brilliance of managing friction is that you don't always need a grand repositioning or a brand rewrite. You need the subtle architecture of flow to run clean. Every second a guest doesn't think counts. Every hesitation costs belief. Every restart counts as effort.

The brain resists effort. Behavioral economists like Daniel Kahneman have proven humans default to the path of least resistance. This is the Principle of Least Effort. When your system forces resistance—cognitive or physical—guests drop off. Restaurants live in urgency. They exist in time scarcity. They serve distracted guests. The Friction Tax hits harder here than almost anywhere else.

This is why data must be your tool of confrontation and not confirmation.

Most brands misuse data. They pull metrics that confirm the story they want to tell. They filter out the ones that challenge their plans. That is the Bias Loop at its worst. When you only surface the numbers that support your decisions, you build a house on sand. You risk the backlash that comes when the guest turns away and your dashboards still look pretty.

When you design with data that confronts your assumptions, you build systems that hold under real conditions.

In a guest-first, clarity-driven system, data is the equalizer. It levels the runway between Marketing, Operations, Tech, and Finance. It removes the department-centric narratives and forces the company to respond to reality. When every team sees the same truth, every decision becomes a system alignment instead of a departmental victory.

When data is treated like oxygen, the brand moves faster. Data becomes truth when leadership accepts that truth may discomfort. Data becomes power when departments coordinate around it instead of hiding behind it. Data becomes transformation when it reshapes the system.

The moment you stop building campaigns and start reducing friction is the moment you stop losing guests in silence.

The Unified Data Model

Modern restaurant organizations throw the word "data" around like it is a singular force. They treat it as one thing. One source. One stream of truth. But inside a restaurant ecosystem, data does not live in one place. It lives in three entirely different realities. It exists in three different vantage points. It acts as three different mirrors reflecting the same guest but from angles that rarely align unless you force them to.

There is MarTech. This is the world of marketing analytics. It tracks attribution paths, loyalty engagement, offer lift, churn curves, and campaign momentum. This is where teams study who clicked, who redeemed, who browsed, who disappeared, and who came back. MarTech reveals Intention. It shows the spark that pulls a guest toward the brand and the patterns that keep them in orbit. It answers who and why.

There is OpsTech. This is the world of Point of Sale (POS) behavior. It tracks throughput logs, Kitchen Display System (KDS) timestamps, ticket variability, production flow, labor cadence, and accuracy dips. It measures the operational rhythm of the restaurant. OpsTech reveals Pressure. It shows how the system behaves during peak demand and when the real world bends a process that looked perfect on a slide. It answers how and at what cost.

There is ExperienceTech. This is the world of app analytics. It tracks web flows, browsing friction, search behavior, menu interactions, pickup patterns, device pathways, and the entire digital front door. ExperienceTech reveals the Journey. It shows how guests move, where they hesitate, where they drop, and where the interface either carries them or confuses them. It answers where and when.

Each of these ecosystems tells a fragment of the story. But when they live apart, the story bends.

Marketing looks at its numbers and thinks a campaign fizzled because the creative missed. Ops looks at its numbers and thinks the kitchen stalled because labor was tight. Digital looks at its numbers and thinks the flow is clean because the pathing looks linear on heatmaps.

Everyone walks away convinced they understand the truth. They are all wrong.

When data sits in silos, it distorts reality.

This distortion fuels the Bias Loop we discussed in the previous chapter. Teams retreat into the metrics that validate their department rather than the metrics that explain the experience.

Consider a specific Friday night failure. Marketing sees that engagement fell. They assume weak messaging. OpsTech shows ticket times spiked that week. This made the experience slower. ExperienceTech shows a high rate of cart abandonment.

In silos, Marketing blames the ad agency. Ops blames the schedule. Digital blames the payment gateway. In a unified model, the truth emerges: The campaign was actually highly effective (MarTech). It drove a surge of traffic that hit the kitchen all at once. The kitchen crashed, causing ticket times to balloon (OpsTech). The digital quote-time algorithm adjusted to the kitchen delay, showing guests a 55-minute wait time. The guests saw that wait time and abandoned their carts (ExperienceTech).

The campaign didn't fail. The operations didn't fail. The digital flow didn't fail. The system failed to balance supply and demand. You cannot see that failure without seeing all three data streams at once.

Every team interprets the world through one lens. One filter. One sliver of behavioral truth. And that is how restaurant brands drift.

Unified data is the only way the truth becomes complete.

A unified data model pulls from all three layers and turns fragments into a chain. You begin to see how marketing influences digital behavior. You see how digital behavior raises operational load. You see how operational load sculpts brand perception and return probability. You see the cycle as one continuous motion instead of three disconnected systems fighting for the same guest.

This represents the virtuous cycle most restaurant brands never notice even though it defines their fate every single day.

Marketing shapes Digital. (Intention drives traffic).

Digital shapes Operations. (Traffic becomes production load).

Operations shape the Outcome of Marketing. (fulfillment determines if the guest returns).

You cannot understand one without understanding all three. You cannot optimize one without touching the others. You cannot fix a broken campaign, a broken interface, or a broken kitchen without understanding the friction that passes between them.

A study by McKinsey & Company found that companies that integrate data across these functions are 1.5 times more likely to report revenue growth of at least 10 percent. The value lies in the integration, not the collection.

This is where modern data platforms finally become essential instead of optional. Platforms like Olo's Rails-level analytics, Square's flow analytics, and Google's cross-environment insights do the heavy lifting. Customer Data Platforms (CDPs) like Segment or mParticle are no longer just for e-commerce giants; they are critical for multi-unit restaurant brands. They stitch these ecosystems together. They reveal the invisible links between guest intention, digital navigation, operational performance, and behavioral outcomes.

They expose the chain of micro-interactions that shape revenue, satisfaction, and trust. They give you a way to see not just what happened, but why it happened.

A unified data model becomes the operating model.

Suddenly the brand can ask the questions that actually matter:

Why did digital conversion drop last week? (Was it a UI change or a kitchen throttle?)

Why did pickup satisfaction tank on Fridays? (Was it staffing or packaging failure?)

Which menu items create disproportionate strain at peak hours? (Does the complex salad kill the drive-thru time?)

Which loyalty offers shift long-term behavior instead of creating short-term spikes? (Do free fries create habits or just cost margin?)

Where does the ordering flow lose momentum?

Where does hesitation creep in?

Where do guests silently switch to another brand?

These questions stop being philosophical. They become measurable. Answerable. Actionable.

Starbucks serves as the gold standard here. Their internal "Deep Brew" initiative is not just an AI project. It is a unified data strategy. It looks at weather, inventory, staffing, and customer preference simultaneously. It doesn't just tell the barista what to make; it tells the inventory system what to order and the app what to suggest, based on the operational capacity of that specific store at that specific minute. They don't guess. They know.

When brands unify data, they stop designing for internal logic. They stop operating on instinct alone. They start designing for the reality of how guests actually behave.

And once the data is unified, something else unlocks. Predictive Empathy.

Personalization stops being a gimmick. Prediction stops being a party trick. The brand begins to remove friction in ways that feel natural instead of creepy. It anticipates needs. It matches timing. It shapes the journey with precision. It builds trust by reducing effort at the exact moments where effort decides whether the guest stays or leaves.

Unified data gives the brand the ability to design experiences the brain wants to repeat. Experiences that feel inevitable. Experiences that convert friction into flow and hesitation into habit.

That is when the brand stops fighting for attention and starts earning devotion.

Personalization, Prediction, and Platform Discipline

Personalization in restaurants has been warped into a marketing trick. A party trick. A cheap flourish. Most brands treat it like a novelty they can sprinkle into campaigns. Insert the guest's name here. Push a "Just For You" offer there. Trigger an email based on a guess. None of that is personalization. It is decoration. It adds weight to the experience instead of removing it. True personalization is quiet. Functional. Behavioral. It exists to reduce cognitive effort and accelerate the path to satisfaction.

Personalization is not about showcasing how much data the brand has. It is about using that data to give the guest the next step before they ask for it.

In a real personalization system, relevance becomes the default. The platform anticipates hunger patterns. It recognizes weekday versus weekend behavior. It knows location tendencies, time-of-day preferences, and the likelihood of customization. It can identify whether the guest is on mobile between meetings or at home planning for a family order. It can detect whether they prefer fast pickup, curbside, dine in, drive thru, or delivery. The goal is simple. Reduce the number of decisions before the guest experiences friction.

This is why personalization is efficiency. It is the removal of effort disguised as familiarity. And when restaurants get this right, the impact is massive. McKinsey found that brands using advanced personalization see up to 40 percent higher revenue impact compared to non-personalized experiences. That gain does not come from better messaging. It comes from reduced cognitive drag. When the system helps you decide, you finish the journey.

The digital front door becomes the proving ground for this work. Local cues now matter. A brand cannot treat every city, every neighborhood, every guest like a cloned data profile. Localization becomes a critical layer of personalization. Guests in Brooklyn move differently from guests in Boise. Guests in Los Angeles order differently from guests in Louisville. Climate, commute patterns, cultural rhythm, workday flow, and local preference all shape behavior.

Localizing the digital flow means the system adapts based on context.

If a guest is near a high volume urban store, show the fastest pickup option first.

If they are in a suburban area where curbside dominates, elevate curbside as the primary pathway.

If the region's sales mix leans heavily toward spicy items, surface those categories sooner.

If weather data shows a cold front moving in, shift visibility toward soups, warm bowls, and comfort items.

If foot traffic data predicts a surge in office workers returning to a district, prioritize grab-and-go or high throughput favorites.

Localization is personalization at scale. It makes the system feel alive. The guest feels understood without the brand needing to say a word.

Reservation systems already operate with this clarity, and restaurant brands often overlook the lesson. Hosts armed with reservation profiles can see dietary restrictions, celebration notes, seating preferences, timing habits, and return frequency before the guest walks through the door. That is personalization. Not because it feels fancy, but because it prepares the experience for precision. The host becomes more confident. The service becomes smoother. The guest feels seen because the system removed uncertainty before it appeared.

That same logic belongs inside quick service and fast casual digital flows. A loyalty profile should act like a reservation note. It should tell the system what to surface, what to skip, what to prioritize, and what to hide. It should shape the journey. A guest who always orders the same three things should not need to browse. A guest who experiments should see variety sooner. A guest who orders for four should see bundles and family formats first. A guest who orders late at night should see the items that hold quality best. This is not individuality for the sake of personalization. This is efficiency engineered at scale.

Platforms either enable this or block it. Rigid systems force the guest into predetermined flows because the technology cannot adapt. The brand becomes trapped by its tools. Every pathway becomes generic. Every journey becomes work. Flexible systems adapt to the guest and allow the brand to build flows that behave like intuition. This is why data driven brands make platform choices with behavioral flexibility at the top of the criteria list. They look for systems that allow iteration, segmentation, contextual visibility, real time recommendations, and predictive surfacing. They avoid anything that turns the menu into a static board.

Predictive personalization becomes the ultimate version of this. The system learns the guest's patterns and adjusts the journey before the guest thinks. Predictive engines can identify when someone is on the brink of abandonment and simplify the flow. They can recognize when someone is shopping delivery versus pickup and present only options that accelerate the intention. They can examine time of day, day of week, weather, store volume, and guest behavior to create a journey that feels inevitable. Not clever. Not manipulative. Inevitable.

This removes the single greatest risk in restaurant UX. The Browsing Spiral. The multi-screen wandering that leads to uncertainty. Uncertainty leads to indecision. Indecision leads to abandonment. Predictive personalization breaks that cycle because it eliminates wandering. It focuses the guest on the finish line.

This is the real purpose of personalization. It is not to feel personal. It is to feel fast.

When brands embrace this truth, they stop seeing personalization as a marketing tactic and start treating it as an operational advantage. Personalization strengthens throughput. It strengthens loyalty. It strengthens retention. It strengthens the guest's sense of control. It strengthens the system.

Because everything connects. Data feeds personalization. Personalization shapes behavior. Behavior fuels loyalty. Loyalty fuels predictability. Predictability fuels growth.

Data is the foundation. But data becomes power only when it designs the journey. When it shapes the menu architecture. When it determines the operational sequence. When it guides the digital flow itself.

Case Study: Wing Stop Flies Higher with Data

In this industry, physics is often the enemy. You cannot cheat cook times. A raw chicken wing takes a specific amount of time to cook safely and crisp perfectly. For years, this reality defined Wingstop's ceiling.

Wingstop's product is bone-in chicken. Unlike a burger that cooks in 3 minutes or a taco assembled in 30 seconds, bone-in chicken takes about 18 to 20 minutes to prepare from order to handoff.

In the "Fast Casual" category, an 18-minute wait is an eternity. It creates a friction barrier. Guests who wanted wings for lunch often skipped Wingstop because they didn't have the time budget. The physics of the product was capping the growth of the brand.

Digitizing the Fryer

Most brands would have tried to solve this with marketing ("Order Ahead!") or labor ("Hire more cooks!"). Wingstop solved it with Data Integration.

They realized that the problem wasn't just the cook time; it was the orchestration of the cook time. Orders were coming in from the counter, the app, DoorDash, and UberEats all at once. Tickets would flood the kitchen, creating bottlenecks.

Wingstop invested in a proprietary "Smart Kitchen" system (OpsTech) that integrated directly with their digital ordering channels (ExperienceTech). This wasn't just a screen showing tickets. It was a logic engine.

Virtual Kitchen: The system virtualized the entire order queue. It knew exactly how many wings were in the fryer, how many were being sauced, and how many were pending.

Predictive Throttling: It used this data to quote accurate times to digital guests.

Production Pacing: It told the cooks exactly what to drop and when, batching similar orders (e.g., Lemon Pepper) to maximize fryer efficiency.

Bending Reality

The results of integrating MarTech (orders) with OpsTech (production) were transformative. CEO Michael Skipworth revealed that this system allowed them to reduce wait times from roughly 20 minutes to roughly 10 minutes.

They didn't change the physics of cooking chicken. They removed the operational drag between the order and the fryer.

Throughput exploded. Same-store sales grew consistently because they could process more volume in the same footprint.

New Occasions Unlocked. A 10-minute wait time made Wingstop a viable option for the lunch crowd, a daypart they previously struggled to capture.

The Lesson

Data is not just for reporting; it is for production.

Wingstop treated data as a raw material, just like chicken. By integrating their data streams, they converted "information" (an order) into "action" (a fryer drop) with zero friction.

Fragmented organizations let orders pile up until the kitchen drowns.

Integrated organizations build systems that pace the demand to match the supply.

Wingstop proved that when you let data run the kitchen, you don't just get better reports. You get a faster restaurant.

Key Takeaways: What Leaders Must Know Now

1. Data is not décor. It is confrontation.

Most restaurant leaders are not data driven. They are opinion driven with data used as supporting garnish. Real data work exists to confront assumptions, not comfort them. When data is treated as validation instead of confrontation, the Bias Loop takes over and the organization slides into delusion.

2. The Bias Loop thrives in analysis, not ignorance.

The danger is not in having no data. It is in having data and bending it to match what you already believe. Cherry picked metrics, flattering dashboards, and "research" that confirms a prewritten story are all symptoms of the Bias Loop. That is not analysis. That is narrative dressed up as numbers.

3. Data is the only honest mirror of behavior.

No leader can see the full guest journey anymore. The experience is too fragmented, too fast, too nonlinear. Data is the only thing that shows what guests actually do across the Invisible Journey—from intention to completion—without filters or ego.

4. Friction is the real competitor.

Most guests do not leave because of bad food or louder competition. They leave because of accumulated friction: tiny drags, confusing flows, awkward pickups, surprise fees, and slow handoffs. Friction is silent and invisible unless you are instrumented to see it. Data is how you see it.

5. Friction is patterned, not random.

Friction appears where the brand's internal model contradicts the guest's behavioral model. Marketing adds complexity. Tech adds steps. Ops improvises around both. Those misalignments are measurable. Abandonment, bounce, lag, variability, and silent churn all carry a behavioral signature.

6. MarTech, OpsTech, and ExperienceTech are three partial mirrors.

Each stack tells a different version of reality:

MarTech reveals intention.

OpsTech reveals pressure.

ExperienceTech reveals journey.

Viewed separately, each becomes a distorted truth. Viewed together, they become a full picture of behavior.

7. Unified data is the real operating model.

When these ecosystems sync, brands can finally see how campaigns impact flows, how flows stress operations, and how operational performance alters future demand. Marketing shapes digital. Digital shapes operations. Operations shape the outcome of marketing. Unified data turns that loop into a controllable system.

8. Data gives power only when everyone shares the same truth.

As long as each department uses its own metrics to "prove" its performance, the brand drifts. When everyone works off a unified, cross-functional view, decisions become system decisions, not departmental victories. Data becomes the equalizer.

9. Personalization is not a gimmick. It is effort removal.

Real personalization is not name insertion or "Just For You" lipstick. It is using data to reduce decisions, steps, and uncertainty. It surfaces the next best action before a guest asks for it. Done well, it makes the journey feel inevitable, not clever.

10. Platform discipline is brand discipline.

Rigid platforms lock brands into generic flows and block behavioral design. Flexible, data-literate platforms let restaurants localize experiences, predict needs, automate relevance, and iterate. Tech choices are no longer "IT decisions." They are brand decisions that define whether data can actually shape the journey.

Action Items: What Leaders Must Do Now

1. Redefine the role of data inside the organization.

Formally declare that data exists to challenge decisions, not decorate them. Bake that into leadership language, performance reviews, and planning rituals.

Question to ask in every review: "What did the data tell us that we did not want to hear?"

2. Hunt for the Bias Loop in current reporting.

Audit dashboards, QBR decks, and ad-hoc reports for signs of cherry picking and self-flattering metrics.

Deliverable: A "Bias Report" that calls out where data is being used as justification instead of illumination.

3. Instrument the Invisible Journey.

Map and measure the full path from intention to completion: search → click → browse → configure → checkout → pickup → post-visit behavior.

Task: Identify at least five key drop-off or hesitation points and connect them to specific friction hypotheses.

4. Build a friction index.

Define and track a small set of friction indicators across digital, in-store, and operations: abandonment rates, lag spikes, high-variance ticket times, pickup complaints, loyalty dormancy, etc.

Outcome: A single "Friction Score" reported alongside revenue and traffic.

5. Connect MarTech, OpsTech, and ExperienceTech into one view.

Stop letting each stack live in isolation. Implement a basic unified data model that joins campaign data, digital behavior, and operational performance at the order and store level.

Deliverable: A weekly "Unified Health" view that shows how guest intention, journey, and throughput interact.

6. Establish a cross-functional Data Council.

Create a recurring session where marketing, digital, ops, finance, and IT review unified data together. No separate decks. No separate stories. One shared source of truth.

Rule: The meeting exists to identify system issues, not to defend department performance.

7. Define non-negotiable data questions for every initiative.

Before launching any campaign, feature, layout change, or process shift, require answers to a short list:

– How will we measure friction?

– What behavior are we trying to change?

– What data will tell us if we were wrong?

Result: Fewer "we feel good about it" launches, more "we learned from it" launches.

8. Reframe personalization as an operational project, not a marketing toy.

Task a joint team (marketing, digital, ops) with one goal: use data to reduce guest decisions and taps by a specific percentage.

Examples: Default to likely orders, surface relevant channels by context, localize flows by store type and daypart.

9. Make platform flexibility a core selection criterion.

When evaluating tech, push past the sales demo.

Ask:

– Can we change flows based on context and behavior?

– Can we feed in external data (weather, traffic, local events)?

– Can we test variations quickly without a rebuild?

Choose tools that let data actually shape experience, not just report on it.

10. Turn data-driven wins into cultural stories.

When a friction fix, unified insight, or personalization shift moves behavior, tell that story loudly. Highlight how confronting the data led to better outcomes than following instinct alone.

Goal: Make "the data changed our mind" a badge of honor, not an admission of weakness.

CHAPTER 10

The Digital Front Door

Building apps, web, and other digital touch points the right way

Digital Is Now the First Door Guests Walk Through

There was a time when guests walked through a physical door before they walked through a digital one. That time is gone. Today, the first door a guest enters is the digital door: the website, the app, the search listing, the map tile, the aggregator feed, the kiosk. Digital is no longer an extension of the restaurant. Digital is the restaurant.

This shift happened so gradually that many brands didn't realize they became digital-first companies until the guest behavior data made it impossible to ignore. For most restaurant brands, well over sixty percent of all guest interactions now begin digitally. For many fast-casual and QSR brands, the number pushes even higher.

The physical experience is now the second impression.

Google's research has shown again and again that the majority of food decisions start on Search, Maps, or Social. "Food near me" searches have become the modern equivalent of driving around looking for a neon sign. Even guests who intend to dine in often check menus, wait times, and pricing digitally before stepping foot in the store. The digital front door influences behavior long before the physical one ever gets a chance to impress.

Deloitte's restaurant industry reports consistently highlight that "digital maturity" is now a primary driver of physical foot traffic. A guest who encounters a broken menu link or a slow-loading site on Google Maps simply chooses the next option. The physical restaurant never even knew they lost the sale. The door was locked before the guest ever reached the handle.

Despite this reality, restaurant brands keep calling their websites "marketing channels." They call their apps "engagement platforms." They call their kiosks "ordering tools." None of these definitions are correct.

Digital is not a channel. Digital is not a platform. Digital is not a tool. Digital is the experience.

It is the expression of the brand's clarity, simplicity, and operational truth. It is the behavioral engine that drives selection, order flow, and confidence. When a guest interacts with your app, they are not "engaging with digital." They are ordering lunch. They are solving a problem. To them, the app is the counter. The screen is the menu. The button is the server.

The most critical reality brands must accept is this: guests arrive at digital touchpoints with purpose, not curiosity.

That is what the last two chapters prepared us for. The Messy Middle has already done the heavy lifting. Exploration and evaluation happened upstream on social media, review sites, and group chats. The guest didn't open a website to "learn about the brand story" or "discover the heritage." They opened it because they are hungry, they are in motion, and they have a job to do.

Psychologically, the guest has shifted from a "deliberative mindset" (weighing options) to an "implemental mindset" (executing a task). In this state, the brain filters out anything that does not aid execution. It views distractions not as "content," but as friction.

This is why every unnecessary screen becomes an act of hostility. Every "immersive" homepage video that auto-plays and slows down the load time is a barrier. Every "Join Our Newsletter" popup that covers the "Order Now" button is an obstacle. Every seasonal takeover that interrupts the path is a breach of contract.

The guest does not owe the brand their patience. The brand owes the guest clarity.

Consider the "Cognitive Load" of a hungry human. When blood sugar is low and time is short—the default state of a restaurant guest—decision fatigue sets in rapidly. A website that forces a guest to close a modal, choose a location, and scroll past a hero image just to see the menu adds cognitive weight. It forces the brain to work when it wants to rest.

Restaurant websites and apps collapse when they treat the guest as someone still wandering through a funnel. They design for a "browser." They should be designing for a "buyer."

They succeed when they treat the guest as someone already standing at the register saying, "Here's what I want."

Imagine walking into a physical fast-casual restaurant. You walk up to the counter, ready to order. Suddenly, a marketing manager jumps in front of you and plays a 30-second video about the founder's trip to Italy. Then, another person hands you a form to sign up for email updates. Only then are you allowed to speak to the cashier. You would walk out. Yet, brands do this digitally every single day and wonder why their conversion rates stall.

Leading brands like Domino's and Chipotle understand this shift. Their digital doors are heavy, industrial-grade entrances designed for throughput. They do not clutter the path. They remember who you are. They present your "usual" order immediately. They treat the digital door as a utility, not a billboard. Domino's famously refers to itself as "an e-commerce company that sells pizza." That distinction matters. It changes how they budget, how they build, and how they measure success.

This chapter is about designing for that moment—the moment of intent—with precision, humility, and behavioral intelligence. We must dismantle the idea of the "brochure website" and the "entertainment app." We must replace them with digital architectures that respect the guest's time and the brand's operations.

The digital door is the only door that matters until the order is placed. If you can't get them through that one, the physical door might as well be painted on the wall.

The UX Patterns That Support Behavior

Google's UX guidelines for QSR and retail do not exist because someone at Google felt inspired one afternoon. They exist because billions of behavioral data points revealed the exact same patterns across cultures, cuisines, and markets. When you watch enough people behave digitally, the truth becomes obvious. The brain wants simple paths. The brain wants clear signals. The guest wants to get to the food without detours.

Google's research revealed something profound. Reducing the number of decisions increases conversion far more than increasing the number of features. Cognitive friction slows ordering more than pricing does. Predictability increases trust more than personalization does. Consistency matters more than beauty.

These findings are humbling for brands that invest heavily in aesthetics and promotion. They force the brand to acknowledge that function shapes feeling, not the other way around.

Leading UX research firms like the Nielsen Norman Group and the Baymard Institute have corroborated these findings for years. They call it Jakob's Law: Users spend most of their time on other sites. This means they prefer your site to work the same way as all the other sites they already know. When a restaurant brand tries to reinvent the wheel—changing where the menu lives or how the cart works—they do not delight the user. They confuse them. Confusion kills conversion.

Here are the patterns that matter most. These are not features. They are behavioral truths.

The first action must be obvious. This is not up for debate. Guests land on a page with one expectation: begin the order. The primary Call to Action (CTA)—"Order Now"—should be immediate, central, and unmissable. It should not be buried. It should not be disguised. It should not be wrapped inside a menu or masked by campaign modules.

If the CTA competes with anything, the experience loses. Eye-tracking studies consistently show that users scan in an "F-Pattern." They look at the top left, scan across, and then down the left side. If your primary button sits outside this natural gaze path, you are forcing the user to hunt. Hunting is work. The brain hates work.

Menus must be scannable, not immersive. The modern guest does not browse. They skim. They jump. They anchor to familiar patterns. Categories should follow mental models rather than internal kitchen sequencing. "Burgers" goes before "Desserts." "Popular Items" should appear first.

The brain wants anchors. The menu should not require thought. Research into "Choice Paralysis," famously demonstrated by Sheena Iyengar's jam study, proves that too many options lead to fewer sales. When a digital menu forces a guest to scroll through fifty un-categorized items, the cognitive load spikes. The guest abandons the cart not because they aren't hungry, but because the effort to choose outweighed the desire to eat.

Fewer steps outperform clever steps. Surprise screens, onboarding flows, and storytelling interludes kill momentum. Guests abandon because they sense the brand isn't respecting their time. Google's testing showed that reducing taps directly increases completion rates. This is a simple but wildly ignored insight.

Every tap is a decision point. Every decision point is an exit ramp. The Baymard Institute found that 18 percent of users abandon an order simply because the checkout process was too long or complicated. If you can do it in three taps, never do it in five.

Modifiers must be obvious and optional. Modifier friction stands as one of the biggest hidden killers of conversion. Endless nested options, unclear choices, and mandatory selections with no default create unnecessary cognitive load.

The guest wants completion, not creativity. Behavioral economics teaches us about the Default Effect. People tend to stick with the default option because it requires the least amount of effort. Smart UX sets the most popular configuration as the default. It allows the guest to modify if they wish, but it does not force them to build the sandwich from scratch every time.

Quote times must be honest. Nothing breaks trust faster than a false promise. If the app says "ready in 10 minutes" and the store needs 20, the Customer Experience (CX) collapses. Google's research repeatedly shows that realistic estimates outperform optimistic ones. Trust drives repeat behavior stronger than speed does.

This is the principle of Operational Transparency. When you lie about time, you create anxiety. When you are honest about a delay, you create agency. The guest can choose to wait or come back later. When you steal their agency with a lie, you lose them forever.

Loyalty must feel like a boost, not a barrier. Loyalty prompts placed before the menu act as hostile gates. They turn value into an obstacle. Guests should order first and identify second. Behavior leads identity, not the other way around.

Forcing a "Login or Sign Up" wall before a guest can even see the price of a burger is the digital equivalent of a bouncer stopping you at the door of a fast-food joint. It is absurd. Guest checkout must be the default. Identity should be captured at the end of the transaction as a utility ("Save this order for next time?") rather than a requirement.

Search behavior must be respected. Most guests land on your site from a specific query. They search for "menu," "nearest location," "order pickup," or "hours." If your site does not answer these queries instantly, the guest leaves. Google calls these "atomic needs." They shape the entire experience.

If a guest searches "Gluten-free menu" and lands on a homepage playing a generic brand video, the site has failed. The site must answer the atomic need immediately.

These patterns are not opinions. They are laws. They are backed by tens of thousands of hours of UX observation and millions of behavior points. Brands that break them are not "creative." They are unclear.

Restaurant leaders often resist these patterns because they feel generic. They fear that consistency will make their brand "look like everyone else."

Consider the door handle. Almost every door handle in the world looks and functions roughly the same way. This is not because architects lack creativity. It is because when you approach a door, you want to open it, not figure it out. The door handle is a convention that allows you to enter the room.

Your digital ordering flow is the door handle. It should not be a puzzle. It should be a convention.

Consistency does not erase identity. It reveals it. It gives the brand a clean surface to express what makes it distinct without forcing the guest to dig for it. The brand's visuals, tone, and personality belong upstream in the Exploration phase. The ordering flow belongs to the guest.

When Digital and Physical Must Match

The digital front door has become the most misunderstood part of the modern restaurant experience. Too many brands still treat it like a separate universe. They view it as a sandbox where marketing paints, product teams tinker, and UX designers optimize screens without ever touching the physical world that must deliver the promise.

But the digital front door does not live on an island. It is welded to the kitchen. It is welded to the line. It is welded to the expo station, the pickup shelf, the drive-thru queue, the labor model, the prep rhythm, the choke points, the training, and the brutal reality of a Saturday night rush.

Digital makes the promise. Physical must keep it. When those two worlds drift apart even slightly, the guest feels the snap.

The kitchen does not run on code; it runs on physics. It has finite capacity. It has finite space. It has finite hands. When a digital interface ignores these physical constraints, it sets the operation up for failure and the guest up for disappointment.

The First Snap: The Quote Time Fiction

The first fracture always shows up in quote times. This is the breaking point every restaurant leader has seen but few acknowledge. Digital systems often generate pickup estimates with logic that feels clean on a screen but collapses in the real world. Ten minutes for a bowl. Fifteen for a platter. Seven for a sandwich. These rules are static abstractions.

The kitchen is reality. The kitchen does not care about abstractions. The kitchen reacts to volume, station load, staffing anomalies, supply variability, dine-in traffic, drive-thru momentum, and the unpredictable rushes that make restaurants what they are.

When digital quote times do not match operational throughput, every guest experiences the same thing: Broken Trust.

Behavioral science tells us that the pain of waiting is defined by the gap between expectation and reality. Maister's Laws of Service dictate that "Unexplained waits are longer than explained waits" and "Uncertain waits are longer than known waits." When an app says 6:15 PM and the food comes out at 6:25 PM, the guest feels lied to. They will tolerate slow. They will not tolerate inaccuracies.

This is why integrated forecasting has become the backbone of brands that treat digital with seriousness.

Panera Bread poured years into predictive prep systems to align digital promises with kitchen capacity. They understood that accurate capacity management was a marketing tool.

Starbucks built real-time load balancing into their mobile ordering engine because stores were drowning under mismatched digital demand. They realized that "throttling" orders was better than ruining the experience.

Chipotle invested in machine learning to balance digital and in-store firepower. They created the "Smarter Pickup Times" logic, which dynamically adjusts promise times based on the exact items in the cart and the current load on the Digital Makeline.

These brands learned the same lesson: a broken quote time erodes loyalty faster than a slow but honest one. Accuracy is empathy at scale.

The Second Fracture: The Pickup Anxiety

The second fracture appears in pickup. Pickup is the final mile of the digital journey, yet it is often treated like a footnote. Brands obsess over ordering flows and ignore the moment that determines whether the entire experience worked.

Pickup is where sentiment forms. Pickup is where clarity becomes felt.

When a guest arrives and cannot tell where to go, who to talk to, whether to check in, whether their order is ready, or whether they should wait or wander, the system collapses. This creates the "Lobby Head Swivel"—that moment of social anxiety where a guest stands in the middle of the room looking around, feeling foolish. No amount of UX precision can save an unclear pickup environment.

Pickup must be unmistakable. Clear zones. Clear signage. Clear shelf logic (is it alphabetical or chronological?). Clear handoff roles. Clear lines of sight. Clear staff accountability.

This is operational, yes, but it is fundamentally digital because digital sets the expectation. If the flow says "grab and go," the shelf must behave like grab and go. If the flow says "meet at counter," someone must be at the counter. Any gap becomes emotional friction. The guest doesn't blame operations. They blame the brand. And they should.

The Third Fracture: The Drive-Thru Collision

The third fracture appears in drive-thru integration. Drive-thru is no longer a channel. It is a battlefield. Volume exploded after 2020 and never returned to pre-surge patterns. Restaurants now run dine-in, walk-in pickup, dedicated pickup shelves, delivery courier lanes, mobile drive-thru, standard drive-thru, and curbside—all at once.

Without orchestration, these channels collide like traffic without signals. Digital orders get injected into drive-thru windows with no awareness of physical queue length. The drive-thru queue backs up and delays digital pickup. Digital prep pulls staff from dine-in expo. The entire system becomes a chain reaction of small delays that compound into chaos.

The brands that shine here are the ones that treat drive-thru like choreography.

Chick-fil-A is the masterclass. Their digital front door aligns perfectly with their physical operations. Guests select mobile drive-thru. The system predicts arrival using geofencing. Line busters with tablets verify names, ensure accuracy, and keep the queue flowing without hesitation. The handoff is fast because the prediction was right. The lanes are orchestrated because the digital promise connected directly to the operational flow.

Chick-fil-A doesn't win drive-thru because of food alone. They win because of alignment. Digital tells the truth. Operations delivers it. That consistency becomes trust. Trust becomes frequency.

The Fourth Fracture: The Loyalty Checkpoint

The fourth fracture appears in loyalty redemption. Redemption is the moment the brand says, "We recognize you." It should feel effortless. Invisible. Seamless.

Yet most brands turn redemption into a chore. They force the guest to open the app, find a QR code, brighten their screen, and hold it up to a scanner that doesn't work on the first try. The line stops. The cashier sighs. The guest feels like a burden.

If the flow slows the line, the staff must intervene. If the staff must intervene, the guest becomes a problem to solve instead of a valued regular. Redemption becomes friction. And friction becomes distance. Redemption should enhance throughput, not drag it. It should behave like a reward, not a negotiation.

Operational Truth Shapes Digital Design

Digital design must reflect operational truth. Operational truth must shape digital design. That is the heartbeat of alignment. That is the heartbeat of the digital front door.

Real-world standouts prove this. Sweetgreen built its digital channels around pickup predictability, investing in dedicated makelines to protect quote integrity. They designed the physical store with shelving that matches the volume their app is capable of generating. Domino's invested in delivery GPS transparency because it understood that perceived waiting is often more painful than actual waiting. They didn't just build a map; they connected the map to the driver's movement, closing the loop between digital promise and physical reality.

And this brings us to Personalization. The next frontier of the digital front door.

Personalization only works when it reduces effort. When it makes the journey feel inevitable. When it removes decisions instead of adding them. And all of that only becomes possible when digital knows what operations can actually support.

A personalized experience that operations cannot fulfill is worse than no personalization at all. Imagine an app suggesting a milkshake because it knows you love dairy, but the shake machine is down at that specific location. The personalization engine says "Yes," but the operational reality says "No." The result is frustration. True personalization requires inventory awareness. It requires operational awareness.

The final section exposes the enemy that destroys all of this: the Shortcut Trap. The temptation to adopt rigid systems and out-of-the-box templates that promise convenience but destroy clarity. Systems that force the guest into friction. Systems that break under real volume. Systems that sever the connection between digital and physical.

That is where the digital front door rises or falls. That is where brands choose scale or stagnation.

Avoiding the Convenience Trap

The Convenience Trap stands as one of the most seductive failures in the restaurant world because it hides behind the mask of safe shortcuts. It always begins with the same line, spoken in a boardroom filled with anxiety about falling behind competitors: "We need a digital ordering solution, and we need it quickly."

Leadership says it with urgency. Vendors hear it with opportunity. The market responds with a parade of promises. Turnkey systems. All-in-one platforms. Rapid deployment. Prebuilt UX flows. Loyalty baked in. AI-driven recommendations. Menu templates ready to go by Friday.

The pitch feels effortless. The demo feels polished. The timeline feels achievable. But convenience at the start almost always becomes complexity at scale.

Shortcuts rarely fail instantly. If they did, no one would buy them. They fail slowly. Quietly. Invisibly. They fail in the gaps between intention and execution. They represent what software engineers call Technical Debt. You borrow time today by making a quick, messy decision, but you pay interest on that decision forever in the form of friction, bugs, and limitations.

Out-of-the-box systems impose someone else's logic on your experience. They shape your menu around their database architecture. They shape your kitchen sequencing around their generic constraints. They shape your modifiers around their rigid templates. They shape your pickup flow around their assumptions. They shape your timing logic around what their engineers thought restaurants should be, not what your restaurant actually is.

Because the system feels functional in the beginning, brands do not see the problem until the system becomes the bottleneck.

The Anatomy of a Shortcut

This is how it happens. The vendor demo shows a clean ordering journey. It hides the rigidity underneath.

Menu Architecture: You cannot reorder categories to match your new LTO strategy. You are stuck with their alphabetized list.

Modifier Logic: You cannot simplify modifiers. If a guest wants "Light Ice," they have to click three times because the system doesn't support a toggle.

Prep Logic: You cannot adjust prep logic for complex items. A salad takes as long as a soup in the system's eyes, wrecking your quote accuracy.

Loyalty Mechanics: You cannot refine loyalty mechanics. You want to reward frequency; the system only knows how to reward spend.

Workflow: You cannot tailor the experience to how your staff actually works.

The ticket prints in a format that confuses the line cook, slowing down the expo window.

Every "quick win" becomes a permanent constraint. And constraints compound. A single rigid decision becomes a structural limitation. A structural limitation becomes operational friction. Operational friction becomes guest frustration. Guest frustration becomes drop-off. Drop-off becomes drift. Drift becomes loss.

This is why shortcuts are the most expensive mistake a restaurant can make. You pay for them every day in ways no ledger can capture. You pay for them in the customer who abandons their cart because the login flow was broken. You pay for them in the drive-thru line that stalls because the mobile order integration failed.

The Post-2020 Graveyard

Look at the brands that suffered early digital friction in the post-2020 surge. Many adopted generic "White Label" systems just to survive the moment. They bought the shortcut. When volume stabilized, those systems became anchors.

They struggled to update UX to match modern standards. They struggled to adapt flows for new channels like curbside pickup. They struggled to optimize for pickup accuracy because the software wasn't aware of the physical shelf capacity. They struggled to unify loyalty and ordering into one system, creating a disjointed experience where guests had to sign in twice.

The more the brand grew, the more the system resisted.

Meanwhile, the brands that invested in flexible frameworks thrived. Chick-fil-A built their digital infrastructure to reflect their operational choreography. They never forced the kitchen to bend to digital. They forced digital to bend to the kitchen. Their mobile drive-thru experience is unmatched because the system utilizes geofencing technology to trigger prep only when the guest is close. The system reflects how the operation actually works. Their line busters with tablets are not a gimmick. They are a digital extension of operational truth. Data flows in both directions. Digital predicts. Operations confirms. The system adjusts in real time. That is the opposite of a shortcut. That is long-term structural clarity.

Chipotle, facing explosive digital growth, refused to let their systems dictate their behavior. They built a dedicated "Digital Makeline" because the digital demand required operational expansion. They used machine learning to match quotes to real prep times, analyzing millions of transactions to understand exactly how long a burrito takes to make at 7:00 PM on a Friday versus 2:00 PM on a Tuesday. They avoided rigidity by building infrastructure that could grow with them. Not bend them.

Panera built predictive load modeling so the digital flow would not over-promise. Starbucks redesigned its mobile ordering logic to reflect real store capacity, introducing the ability to turn off mobile ordering at specific stores when the barista team was overwhelmed. Domino's built the "Pizza Tracker" not as a marketing gimmick but as a transparency tool rooted in actual sensor data from the oven.

These brands avoided shortcuts because they understood the cost of mismatched systems. They invested in adaptability because adaptability creates longevity.

The Choice: Features vs. Adaptability

Every rigid system eventually hits a wall. Every flexible system grows with the brand.

This is the truth most leaders resist because the shortcut promises speed. Yet speed at implementation becomes friction at scale. A shortcut locks the brand into someone else's assumptions. Someone else's constraints. Someone else's architecture. Your brand becomes a tenant in a structure you did not design.

The real cost of shortcuts is not the subscription fee or the setup cost. The real cost is Friction. Friction your guests feel when the app crashes. Friction your teams absorb when the KDS lags. Friction your system cannot escape because the code is closed.

Shortcuts force improvisation. Staff must fill the gaps the system cannot interpret. They create inconsistency across locations. They produce drift as markets grow. They erode trust one glitch, one delay, one confusing pickup moment at a time.

The Shortcut Trap destroys clarity because clarity depends on control. When your system is rigid, you lose control. The platform dictates your UX. The platform dictates your ops logic. The platform dictates your menu architecture. The platform dictates your redemption pathways. And when your platform dictates your brand, your brand becomes generic. You lose the advantage you fought to earn. You lose the soul of your system. You lose the ability to scale with intention.

The strongest digital brands do not choose platforms for features. Features age. Features plateau. Features become noise.

Strong brands choose platforms for adaptability. They choose systems (often "Headless" or "API-first" architectures) that let them align digital flow with operational flow. They choose systems that let them adjust timing logic to match prep reality. They choose systems that allow real personalization, localization, segmentation, and prediction. They choose systems that allow refinement without structural overhaul. They choose systems that empower innovation instead of blocking it.

Digital is the front door. But alignment is the building. A flawless front door cannot save a collapsing structure. But a strong structure can elevate any front door.

Convenience weakens the structure. Clarity strengthens it.

Case Study: Cava Cracked Convenience

The restaurant industry is addicted to the concept of "Asset Light." Wall Street loves it. Private Equity demands it. The logic is simple: Don't own the stores. Don't employ the line cooks. Just build a brand, sell the franchise rights, and collect the royalties. It is the ultimate shortcut to scale. You get the dots on the map without the headache of the operations.

When CAVA began its ascent to becoming the dominant Mediterranean fast-casual brand, the pressure to franchise was immense. The "Chipotle of Mediterranean" lane was wide open, and speed was the presumed winner.

The Siren Song of Speed

In the late 2010s and early 2020s, the playbook for growth was set.

Quiet Killers

Franchise aggressively: Let other people put up the capital.

Ghost Kitchens: Open "virtual" locations in warehouses to capture delivery volume without paying for prime real estate.

This is the Convenience Trap in action. It promises scale without friction. It promises revenue without responsibility.

Rejecting the Playbook

CAVA's leadership, led by CEO Brett Schulman, looked at the "Asset Light" model and saw a trap. They realized that in a category defined by fresh ingredients and assembly-line customization, Operations is the Brand.

If you franchise, you lose control of the culture. If you lose control of the culture, you lose the consistency of the bowl. If you lose the bowl, you lose the guest.

CAVA chose the "hard road."

No Franchising: They own every single location. They employ every single general manager.

No Ghost Kitchens: Schulman famously called ghost kitchens a "shiny penny" that distracted from the core purpose of community and connection. He argued that a brand that disappears into a warehouse loses its soul.

MVC (Mission, Values, Competencies)

Instead of spending energy selling franchises, CAVA spent energy building an internal operating system for talent called MVC (Mission, Values, Competencies).

They treated their General Managers (GMs) as the most important people in the company, not as interchangeable parts. They built a training pipeline that incentivized GMs to act like owners, offering stock and clear career paths. They centralized food production in their own production centers (for dips and spreads) to ensure that the hummus tasted the same in Boston as it did in Los Angeles.

They didn't try to scale the store count first. They scaled the system first.

The IPO and The Moat

In June 2023, CAVA went public. It was one of the most successful restaurant IPOs in recent history. As of late 2024, the stock has soared, and the brand is valued at multiples higher than its franchised competitors.

Why? Because the market realized that CAVA had built a moat.

Competitors who franchised rapidly are now struggling with inconsistent food quality, franchisee revolts, and brand dilution.

CAVA controls its destiny. When they want to roll out a new steak item, they don't have to negotiate with 500 franchisees. They just do it. When they want to change a digital flow, they deploy it instantly.

Takeaway

The Convenience Trap tells you that "owning operations" is a burden. It tells you to offload the hard work to someone else.

CAVA proved that Owning Operations is the Strategy.

Franchising is a shortcut to size, but a barrier to quality.

Ghost Kitchens are a shortcut to reach, but a barrier to connection.

By refusing the shortcuts, CAVA built a brand that isn't just big; it's dense. They didn't just plant flags; they built foundations. In a nonlinear world, the brand that controls its own quality is the only brand that is safe.

Key Takeaways: What Leaders Must Know Now

1. Digital is not a channel. It is the restaurant.

For most guests, the first door is now digital: search, maps, apps, aggregators, kiosks. That experience is not "marketing." It is the primary expression of your brand's clarity, speed, and operational reality. If digital fails, the brand fails.

2. Guests arrive with intent, not curiosity.

By the time someone hits your site or app, exploration and evaluation already happened. They are hungry. They are in motion. They have a job to do. Treating them like they are still "learning about the brand" is delusional. You design for intent, not wandering.

3. Every extra screen is hostility.

Immersive videos, full-bleed campaigns, loyalty gates, and storytelling detours all send the same message: "Our needs matter more than your time." The guest does not owe you attention. You owe them a clean path.

4. UX patterns are not "best practices." They are behavioral laws.

Clear first action, scannable menus, fewer steps, sane modifiers, honest quotes, respectful loyalty flows, and atomic needs (menu, order, locations, hours) are not optional. They are proven behaviors. Breaking them is not creativity. It is confusion.

5. Digital promises are welded to physical reality.

The app is not separate from the kitchen or the line. Quote times, prep logic, pickup flows, drive thru choreography, and loyalty redemption all live at the intersection of digital and ops. When those two drift, trust snaps.

6. Quote time accuracy is a trust contract.

Guests can forgive slow. They do not forgive lies. A "ready in 10" that turns into 20 erodes belief faster than an honest 20 that delivers on time. Accuracy is empathy at scale.

7. Pickup is the final exam.

You can't polish your way past a chaotic pickup experience. If guests do not know where to go, what to do, or who is accountable, the entire journey feels broken. Pickup is sentiment formation. If that moment is unclear, everything upstream becomes forgettable.

8. Drive thru and multi-channel flows live or die on orchestration.

Drive thru, curbside, walk-in, shelves, courier pickup, and dine in all run at once. Without integrated logic, they cannibalize each other. The winners treat drive thru and off-prem like choreography, not chaos.

9. Loyalty must accelerate the experience, not interrupt it.

Redemption and identification should feel like lubrication, not sand in the gears. When loyalty slows lines, confuses staff, or adds steps, it becomes an anti-perk.

10. The Shortcut Trap is the most expensive "savings" you'll ever buy.

Rigid, out-of-the-box systems feel cheap and fast at implementation, then punish you at scale. They lock you into someone else's menu logic, UX flows, and operational assumptions. The real cost is friction you can't fix.

11. Flexibility is the new non-negotiable feature.

Strong brands choose platforms that can bend to their operations, not platforms that demand operations bend to them. Adaptability, configurability, and behavioral control outlast any shiny feature list.

12. Digital is the door, alignment is the building.

You can have a beautiful app and a gorgeous site, but if operations, timing, and flows don't align, the structure collapses. Digital is only as strong as the system it represents.

Action Items: What Leaders Must Do Now

1. Rewrite how you define "digital" internally.

Stop calling your website a marketing channel and your app an engagement tool.

Action:

Publish a one-page internal statement: "Digital is the restaurant." Use it to reset expectations for every department.

2. Make "Begin Order" the undisputed primary action.

Audit your homepages, apps, kiosks, and map-linked experiences.

Action:

- Move "Order" or "Start Order" to the most prominent, central position.
- Strip competing hero modules that distract from that action.
- If the first step is not obvious in under two seconds, you are losing people.

3. Ruthlessly cut steps in the ordering flow.

Count every tap from landing to checkout.

Action:

- Remove decorative interstitials, forced onboarding, and non-essential fields.
- Set a maximum tap count target for primary journeys (e.g., "from tap to confirm in X steps").

- Fewer steps = more completed orders. Treat every extra tap like a tax.

4. Fix menu architecture for scanning, not storytelling.

Review your digital menu the way a rushed guest does.

Action:

- Reorganize categories around mental models (popular items, quick picks, core categories) instead of back-of-house logic.
- Use plain language, clear photos, and smart defaults for modifiers.
- If a new guest has to think to find basics, you've already failed.

5. Turn quote times into a cross-functional contract.

Connect kitchen reality to digital promises.

Action:

- Pull actual ticket time data by daypart and product type.
- Adjust quote logic to be realistic for peak and off-peak.
- Create an escalation path when tickets begin to drift beyond promised timing.
- If operations cannot influence quote logic, your system is lying by design.

6. Redesign pickup like it is the most important moment in the journey. Because it is.

Walk the pickup path as a first-time guest.

Action:

- Create clear signage from entrance to pickup zone.
- Standardize shelf logic (alpha, time-based, order number) and label it visibly.
- Establish clear staff ownership for digital handoff.

- Your goal: zero spoken questions required to complete pickup.

7. Map and orchestrate all fulfillment channels together.

List every way an order can be fulfilled across your system: dine in, walk-in, drive thru, mobile drive thru, curbside, courier pickup, shelves, etc.

Action:

- Diagram how digital injects orders into each line.
- Identify collision points where channels steal labor, space, or attention from each other.
- Adjust staffing and flows so digital promises do not break in physical queues.

8. Clean up loyalty flows so they feel like a boost, not a barrier.

Test every touchpoint where loyalty appears: sign-up, earn, redeem, identify.

Action:

- Move loyalty prompts after menu exposure or at checkout, not as gatekeeping at the start.
- Make redemption one tap or one scan, never a negotiation.
- Reward should equal relief, not complexity.

9. Audit your tech stack for Shortcut Trap symptoms.

Make a brutally honest list of where your current systems block basic improvements.

Ask:

Can we change menu structure ourselves?

Can we adjust flows without a dev ticket?

Can we localize options by store, daypart, or channel?

If the answer is "no" to most of these, you're in the Trap.

10. Create a platform selection scorecard based on flexibility, not features.

Before you sign the next platform contract:

Criteria to score:

Ability to adapt flows to operations

Control over quote logic

Menu and modifier configurability

Support for contextual personalization and localization

Ease of testing and iteration

Use this scorecard to kill "fast and rigid" options early.

11. Turn "alignment checks" into a required step for any digital change.

No new UX pattern, campaign, or digital feature goes live without operational signoff.

Action:

- Build a simple checklist: Does digital reflect prep reality? Pickup reality? Drive thru reality? Staffing reality?
- Include ops in the approval loop, not as an after-the-fact patch crew.

12. Tell the no-shortcuts story internally. Often.

Use real examples (yours or others) where shortcuts created long-term pain.

Action:

- Share case studies where rigid tools blocked growth and where flexible systems enabled it.
- Celebrate projects where you chose the "harder but right" tech path and it paid off.
- You're rewiring instinct: from "fast is good" to "flexible is mandatory."

CHAPTER 11

The Restaurant Brand Operating Model

The End of Departments and the Rise of Integrated Organizations

Killing the Siloed Leadership & Fragmented Execution Killer requires killing your comfort first. Departments behaving like fortified camps guarding their own land must end. Most restaurant organizations still arrange themselves like an office park from 2004 where Marketing launches campaigns, Technology builds systems, Operations keeps the lights on, and Finance polices the budget. Each group stays busy defending its territory, priorities, and version of how the business functions. They call this structure "focus." In reality, it is an antique map of a world that no longer exists.

Inside these departmental walls, every team develops its own language and rituals. They build their own tools. They adopt their own processes. They enforce their own timelines. They justify decisions by referencing the needs of their group rather than the needs of the guest. They hold meetings to align, yet those meetings rarely align anything. They share plans, yet those plans rarely integrate. What most leaders call collaboration is nothing more than a baton pass. Work moves in a straight line from one silo to the next while accumulating assumptions, constraints, and debris. By the time it reaches the guest, what was once a simple idea now carries the fingerprints of every department that touched it plus the friction of every department that resisted it.

This archaic model would be survivable if guest behavior remained linear. The modern guest journey refuses to move in a straight line. It loops. It jumps. It moves erratically from digital to on-premise to word of mouth and back to digital. The old model is hostile to reality. A nonlinear world requires an organization designed for nonlinear execution. Restaurant brands lose with department-first thinking. They must transform themselves into integrated experience organizations.

Experience organizations treat marketing, technology, operations, finance, and design as interdependent expressions of a single organism. One circulatory system. One nervous system. One brain making decisions for the same body. Fully integrated.

Mechanics drive this necessity. When a guest interacts with a brand, they experience one chain of events. They see one promise, one path, and one payoff. If the internal machine is fragmented, the guest will feel it. They feel the seams. They feel the handoffs. They feel the moments when one department failed to talk to another. Every internal boundary eventually becomes an external flaw that cracks the Projection layer the guest uses to identify with the brand.

Restaurant brands that truly integrate make the tough leadership move to dismantle departmental autonomy. Autonomy breeds protectionism. Protectionism breeds territorial behavior. Territorial behavior kills experience coherence. Leaders must un-encamp their teams. They must remove the instinct to fortify a department's identity, defend its backlog, and lobby for its agenda. Teams must stop asking what their department needs to succeed. They must ask what the guest experience requires and how the organization collectively makes that happen.

This rewiring of the operating model anchors decisions in behavioral impact rather than departmental preference. Priorities shift toward the moments that matter instead of the moments a department happens to own. Work stops moving in lanes and starts moving in loops. The organization behaves less like a series of conveyor belts and more like a cross-functional war room.

The shift feels uncomfortable at first, yet the payoff is profound. Brands that break down departmental walls find that internal friction begins to evaporate. Disagreements become productive instead of political. Teams solve for outcomes instead of protecting opinions. Decisions accelerate because the right people are involved from the start rather than being pulled in at the end. Marketing stops crafting messages in isolation. Technology stops shipping features no one else understands. Operations stops making on-prem changes without considering upstream impact. Teams stop building in private and start building in partnership.

Most importantly, the brand stops lurching between disconnected visions. It gains coherence. It gains rhythm. It gains speed without chaos. The brand's Archetype finally has a clear channel to direct behavior across the entire ecosystem.

Leaders often hesitate here out of a fear of losing control. The opposite happens. When silos fall, clarity rises. Alignment becomes tangible. The organization begins to move with a shared pulse instead of departmental beats stepping on each other. Protective instincts soften because people now see the brand as something they co-own rather than something they defend from one another.

Survival demands this integration. The nonlinear guest journey demands a nonlinear organization capable of adapting as fluidly as its guests do. Insights in marketing must automatically shape product decisions. Digital intelligence must naturally inform operational adjustments. Operations feedback must instantly influence messaging, throughput planning, and technology needs. These shifts occurring independently fractures the experience. These shifts occurring together makes the experience unstoppable.

This is the operating transformation the entire book has been pointing toward. Everything before this chapter exposed the forces that sabotage brands from the inside. This is where the cure begins. Building a modern restaurant brand requires leaders willing to dismantle the outdated structures that make fragmentation inevitable. They must replace them with systems, rituals, incentives, and rhythms that turn integration from aspiration into operating reality.

The Rhythms That Hold Integrated Organizations Together

Integration doesn't happen because leadership puts the word "collaboration" on a slide deck. It happens because the organization installs the rhythms, cadences, and rituals that make unified work unavoidable. Without these rhythms, even the most well-intentioned teams drift back into their familiar silos. With them, alignment becomes the path of least resistance.

The most effective restaurant organizations share the same foundational rhythms. They plan the work together, not in departmental drafts. They evaluate performance together, not through isolated dashboards. They launch initiatives together, not as staged handoffs. Their meetings aren't check-ins as much as they're co-creation spaces where each team brings a piece of the puzzle.

The Quarterly Experience Sync

Quarterly planning is one of the rituals that makes the biggest impact. In fragmented organizations, quarterly planning is a departmental exercise. Marketing sets campaign schedules based on holidays. Technology sets roadmaps based on backlog. Operations sets staffing and store-level priorities based on budget. These plans meet for the first time weeks or months later, usually when a conflict arises that forces a compromise.

Integrated organizations scrap that approach entirely. They hold joint planning sessions where one singular question drives the agenda: "What experience improvements matter most this quarter?"

That question reframes everything. It forces teams to anchor around behavioral impact instead of legacy responsibilities. It turns priorities into shared commitments. It forces resource decisions into the open, eliminating the shadow politics that often accompany cross-team tradeoffs. If Marketing wants to launch a complex LTO, Operations has to sign off on the labor model in the room. If Tech wants to refactor the checkout flow, Marketing has to understand the temporary dip in conversion. It aligns timelines from the start. It makes collaboration proactive rather than reactive.

The Weekly Pulse: Evaluating System Health

Weekly or biweekly experience reviews are just as essential. They don't focus on department KPIs alone. They focus on the health of the system.

In a siloed organization, Marketing reports on "Impressions," Ops reports on "Labor," and Tech reports on "Uptime." Everyone gets a gold star, yet the brand might be failing.

Integrated reviews look at the connective tissue. They look at Digital Conversion (Marketing + Tech). They look at Quote-Time Accuracy (Tech + Ops). They look at Pickup Variability (Ops + CX). They look at Loyalty Engagement relative to Throughput (Marketing + Ops).

These reviews expose friction early, long before it becomes expensive or public. They shift the role of data inside the organization. In siloed brands, data is interpreted through departmental filters. Integrated organizations create shared dashboards that reveal behavioral truth across the entire system. They interpret data together. They disagree together. They solve together.

The Launch Gate: Co-Owned Initiatives

Integration also requires shared rituals around launch. In traditional organizations, a new campaign or feature or operational adjustment is "owned" by one team and "supported" by others. But ownership is the wrong metaphor. Launches in integrated organizations are co-owned.

No initiative goes live without cross-functional validation. This is the "Launch Gate."

Marketing cannot launch without Digital Readiness (Are the assets loaded? Is the tracking active?).

Digital cannot launch without Operational Feasibility (Can the kitchen handle the volume? Is the KDS updated?).

Operations cannot adjust without Digital Compatibility (Does the new station layout match the app flow?).

These safeguards eliminate friction before it hits the guest. They prevent the classic "Marketing sold something Operations can't make" scenario.

Case Study: Due' Cucina and the Science of Consistency

Scaling a restaurant concept is usually a test of logistics. For Filippo Fiori and Davide Macchi, founders of Due' Cucina, it was a test of physics.

Fiori and Macchi were nuclear scientists in Italy before they were restaurateurs. They approached pasta not as a craft, but as a chemistry equation. In their first location in Seattle, the equation worked. The environment was controlled. The output was consistent.

Then they expanded to Texas.

When Variables Collide

The expansion broke the equation. Texas introduced variables the Seattle model hadn't accounted for: aggressive heat, intense humidity, and altitude changes.

The Environment: Higher ambient temperatures changed how the water held heat.

The Volume: Different batch sizes and absorption rates for different pasta shapes created chaos during the rush.

The "al dente" bite—the singular brand promise of authentic Italian pasta—began to drift.

The SOP Trap

Most operators react to drift by adding rules. Due' Cucina initially tried this. They lined the stations with thermometers. They created complex manual charts to guide cooks through the variables ("If water is X and batch is Y, cook for Z").

It worked on paper. It failed on the line. The cognitive load was too high. During a Friday night rush, no cook has the bandwidth to cross-reference a physics chart. The system relied on human heroics, and heroics don't scale.

The Algorithm as Head Chef

Fiori and Macchi stopped acting like operators and started acting like scientists again. They realized they couldn't train the variable out of the human; they had to build the variable into the system.

They built a proprietary app that acted as the kitchen's brain.

The Inputs: Real-time water temperature recovery rates, specific pasta shapes, current batch size, and environmental conditions.

The Output: A precise, dynamic countdown for every single basket.

Codifying Consistency

The app removed the guesswork. Cooks no longer had to "feel" the pasta or interpret complex charts. They simply followed the system.

Drift Vanished: The pasta returned to perfect consistency, whether in rainy Seattle or humid Texas.

Training Simplified: You didn't need a pasta expert on the line; you needed someone who could follow the tool.

Takeaway

Integrated organizations do not force humans to compensate for a complex system. They build systems that absorb the complexity so the human can focus on execution.

Due' Cucina treated drift as data. Instead of writing thicker training manuals (The Bias Loop), they built a tool that synced operational reality with digital intelligence. They didn't just solve a cooking problem; they solved a scaling problem.

What Integrated Brands Actually Measure

Integrated brands measure what matters because they understand that the guest does not experience marketing, operations, or digital as separate teams. The guest experiences a single system. One journey. One chain of behaviors. One promise that either holds together or falls apart. Most restaurant organizations measure the wrong things because they measure in silos. They measure what they want to see instead of what the guest actually feels. And that is how brands drift.

Traditional Key Performance Indicators (KPIs) reward local optimization. Integrated KPIs reward system health.

Siloed optimization is a false win. It happens when a department celebrates success while creating damage somewhere else in the chain. Marketing cheers a spike in website traffic, but digital analytics show those visitors never converted. Operations celebrates faster throughput, but pickup data shows the digital promise couldn't keep up. Technology celebrates 99.99 percent uptime, but store teams beg for relief because the latest feature rollout shredded their workflow.

This is fragmentation disguised as performance.

Integrated brands refuse to celebrate numbers that don't align across the system. They understand what MIT's Center for Information Systems Research has proven repeatedly: organizations that integrate technology, operations, and experience see significantly higher operational performance and customer satisfaction because cross-functional systems reduce friction at every touchpoint. Integrated brands listen to the behavioral truth of their data instead of the flattering illusions of departmental dashboards.

They measure the experience, not the activity. They measure the system, not the silo.

The KPIs That Actually Measure Experience

Performance

Integrated brands gravitate toward a specific set of KPIs because these metrics reveal the lived reality of the guest journey. They reflect behavioral truth. They expose friction. They highlight drift. They unify teams because no department can move these numbers alone.

Here are the KPIs that tell the real story:

Ordering-flow efficiency. How fast does a guest move from intention to order? Every extra tap increases abandonment. Research from the Baymard Institute shows high-friction checkout flows can raise abandonment rates to over 70 percent. The restaurant world is no different. Effort kills intent.

Digital conversion. Traffic means nothing without conversion. Google's restaurant search behavior studies have shown that guests evaluate speed and clarity subconsciously within seconds. Slow-loading menus, unclear categorization, and poor location routing take immediate behavioral tolls.

Pickup consistency. Guests forgive many things. They do not forgive inconsistency. Deloitte's foodservice research found that pickup confusion ranks among the top three sources of negative sentiment in digital restaurant experiences.

Quote-time accuracy. Accurate quotes are a trust signal. A study published in the Journal of Service Management shows perceived wait accuracy plays a stronger role in satisfaction than the actual wait itself. Guests tolerate slow when slow is expected. They reject broken promises.

Ticket-time reliability. Variability is the enemy. Variability creates unpredictability. Unpredictability erodes confidence. Integrated brands track not just average ticket time but spread—the deviation that predicts guest disappointment.

Order accuracy rate. According to the American Customer Satisfaction Index, order errors are the number one driver of negative restaurant sentiment. Accuracy is the most fundamental trust contract in a restaurant brand.

Repeat-order frequency. Repeat behavior is the metric that reveals whether the system works. McKinsey's personalization report found that 78 percent of consumers are more likely to repurchase when the experience aligns with expectations and reduces effort. Frequency is earned, not marketed.

Loyalty redemption friction. When redemption requires staff intervention or introduces awkwardness, retention drops. Paytronix's annual loyalty report shows that guests abandon loyalty programs not because rewards aren't compelling, but because redemption is "too hard" or "doesn't work in-store."

Search-to-order clarity. This spans Google Maps, brand search, local results, and SEO patterns. Harvard's research into digital discoverability shows that restaurants with clear local intent signals see higher conversion simply because guests do not struggle to verify the experience.

Store-level experience satisfaction. This is not a smiley-face survey. It is the cross-reading of digital signals, order accuracy, pickup timing, and repeat patterns. Behavior is the truth. Feedback is commentary.

Each of these KPIs does the same thing: they track what the guest experiences, not what the organization believes.

Experience Objectives and Key Results (OKRs): Where Integration Becomes Measurable

KPIs measure the truth. OKRs change the truth.

Integrated brands use OKRs to align every department around one shared outcome. They do not assign OKRs to individual teams because no single team can improve these metrics. The system improves them, or nothing does.

An integrated OKR looks like this:

Reduce digital abandonment by 12 percent.

This forces Marketing, Digital, Ops, Tech, and even Training into the same conversation. Abandonment is never just a UX issue. It is an intention, clarity, loading-speed, quote-time, and pickup-confidence issue.

Decrease pickup-time variability by 20 percent.

This pushes operations and digital into alignment. Variability usually comes from misaligned quote logic, kitchen load balancing, staffing inconsistencies, and unclear pickup signage.

Increase repeat orders among first-time digital guests by 15 percent.

This requires marketing, product, loyalty, and operations to build the system that earns a second visit. Not a campaign. A system.

Improve accuracy rate by 5 points across all channels.

Accuracy is where digital complexity collides with physical execution. This lifts the entire cross-functional organization.

Integrated OKRs unify the brand around behavior instead of preference. They force the organization to measure the only thing that matters: system performance.

Integrated Organizations Don't Measure Effort. They Measure Reality

One of the clearest markers of an integrated, mature restaurant organization is this: they stop rewarding effort and start measuring truth. Most brands would never admit they measure effort, but you can see it in the dashboards. They count posts. They count campaigns. They count feature releases. They track how many trainings were deployed, how many meetings were held, how many pilots ran, how many assets were shipped. These are activity metrics. They measure motion, not movement. They tell you how hard a team is working, not how well the system is working.

Effort is comforting. It gives every department something to point to. It creates the illusion of progress, even when the guest experience remains unchanged.

Quiet Killers

It protects teams from accountability because it frames success as productivity rather than performance. But in an integrated organization, effort is irrelevant if reality does not change. Guests don't care how many hours went into a flow redesign if the flow still confuses them. They don't care how many campaigns were launched if none of them influence behavior. They don't care how many operational memos hit their franchisees if the dining room still feels disjointed.

Integrated organizations measure reality. They measure clarity. They measure flow. They measure those tiny points of resistance that accumulate into lost revenue, eroded trust, and quiet churn. We call that "friction." They measure how clearly the brand promise is felt at every touchpoint and how consistently the system can deliver on that promise under stress.

This shift from effort to experience requires a different class of KPIs and OKRs. These are not "marketing KPIs," "tech KPIs," or "ops KPIs." They are experience KPIs. They cut across departments because the guest journey cuts across departments. They force teams to align around outcomes instead of activities. And they give leaders one of the most powerful tools they can wield: visibility into the truth.

Experience KPIs fall into four broad categories:

1. Clarity Metrics

These measure how well the brand communicates what it stands for and what it wants the guest to do. This includes message comprehension, call-to-action clarity, menu legibility, and wayfinding ease. If clarity is low, everything else suffers. Confused guests bounce. Confused franchisees improvise. Confused staff execute inconsistently. Clarity is not a branding metric. It is a performance metric.

2. Flow Metrics

Flow metrics measure how efficiently guests move through the system. Order journey completion rates. Checkout velocity. Dwell times. Throughput consistency. Pickup accuracy. Anything that shows whether the brand is helping guests move or slowing them down. Flow is where marketing, digital, and operations truly reveal their interdependence. You cannot fix flow with campaigns. You fix flow by aligning incentives and resolving cross-functional friction.

3. Friction Metrics

Friction is the invisible tax guests pay for a brand's internal dysfunction. It shows up as extra taps, unclear handoffs, poorly sequenced operational steps, multiple logins, or a lack of communication during delays. Friction kills conversion. It kills loyalty. It kills frequency. Measuring friction—and removing it systematically—is one of the most powerful drivers of revenue available to a restaurant brand. But you cannot measure friction from inside a department. You must measure it from the guest's point of view.

4. Trust Metrics

Trust metrics measure whether the brand consistently fulfills its promise. This includes first-order repeat rate, app retention, guest-reported reliability, order accuracy consistency, and the ever-important "Would you return?" indicator. Trust is the scoreboard of experience execution. You cannot spin it. You cannot decorate it. You can only earn it.

When an organization adopts experience KPIs, something remarkable happens: politics weaken. Activities lose their protective armor. The conversation shifts from "We shipped it on time" to "Did it work?" From "We ran the campaign as expected" to "Did it change behavior?" From "Ops completed the rollout" to "Did it actually create a better experience?"

Experience KPIs de-center departments and re-center truth.

They also expose the harsh but liberating reality that no single team owns performance. Marketing cannot drive clarity alone. Tech cannot drive flow alone. Operations cannot reduce friction alone. Trust is a shared responsibility with shared consequences. This is what kills the assumption that departments can operate independently and then stitch their work together at the end. Experience KPIs drag interdependence into the light. They make it impossible for departments to hide behind internal metrics that look good while the guest experience looks bad.

This is why integrated KPIs do more than measure performance. They protect the system.

They act as an immune response. When a decision threatens clarity or flow, the metrics flag the risk. When a new technology introduces friction, the metrics expose it. When a campaign overpromises, the metrics force recalibration. When throughput degrades, the metrics trigger collaboration instead of blame. Experience KPIs discipline the organization. They train teams to ask the right questions earlier. They reveal tradeoffs before they become failures. They keep the brand from wandering into strategies that feel exciting inside the building and fall apart the moment they meet the guest.

Most importantly, experience KPIs make scale possible. A brand can grow from 5 to 15 units with charisma. It can grow from 15 to 50 with hustle. But it cannot grow from 50 to 500 without discipline. It cannot scale if clarity collapses every time new messaging launches. It cannot scale if flow breaks whenever menu complexity increases. It cannot scale if friction compounds with every layer of technology. And it cannot scale if trust erodes quietly while internal dashboards proudly celebrate activity.

Experience KPIs force the truth onto the table. They make reality visible. They give leaders the tools to correct problems early instead of apologizing for them later. They turn integration from a cultural aspiration into a measurable operating model.

These metrics become the foundation for everything that comes next: the roadmap, the sequencing, the resourcing, the decisions that turn a small, promising brand into a large, resilient one. Because integrated organizations do not guess. They do not hope. They measure reality. And then they build on it.

Scaling From 5 to 500: Why Integration Becomes a Compounding Advantage

Scaling from five units to five hundred is not linear growth. It is a metamorphosis. It is a stress test that exposes the truth of your system. It reveals every weak seam.

It punishes every improvisation you once got away with.

When a brand has five units, problems are solved by people. The founder drives to the location, fixes the fryer, retrains the manager, and apologizes to the guest. The brand runs on "Founder's Energy."

When a brand has five hundred units, the founder cannot drive to the problem. Problems must be solved by systems. If the system is broken, the problem multiplies by five hundred.

Scaling is not about planting flags on a map. It is the discipline of teaching your brand to operate in more conditions, with more variables, under more pressure, without bending into something unrecognizable. Most restaurant brands do not fail because their food concept is weak. They fail because their operating system never learned how to hold its shape.

Fragmented Organizations Scale Fragility. Integrated Organizations Scale Strength.

A fragmented brand enters scale with swelling inconsistencies. Because the departments—Marketing, Tech, Ops, Finance—never unified their logic, the cracks widen with every new lease signed.

Stores interpret the playbook differently. Managers in Florida invent their own versions of the experience because the guidance from corporate is ambiguous.

Digital feels distinct. The app feels sharp in one market but clumsy in the next because the UX was never matched to the specific kitchen layouts of the new real estate.

Loyalty logic behaves unpredictably. No one defined the mechanics tightly enough to handle edge cases, so guests get frustrated when rewards don't redeem.

Packaging collapses under volume. It looked great in the boardroom test but gets soggy in the delivery radius of a dense urban center.

Marketing pushes national campaigns the field cannot fulfill. This creates internal friction (angry franchisees) and external disappointment (confused guests).

In fragmented systems, every additional unit is a new doorway through which inconsistency enters.

Guests feel this immediately. They feel it when one store nails the pickup flow and another turns it into an Easter egg hunt. They feel it when digital promises a ready-at-five order and the physical store hands it over at five-fifteen. They feel it when a brand feels premium in the suburbs but chaotic in the city.

Fragmentation creates a fractured brand reality. A guest can interact with the same brand twice in one day and feel like they visited two different companies. Nothing destroys trust faster.

Integrated Brands Behave Differently

Integrated brands build differently because they understand that they are building a product, not just a menu. Integration is not alignment meetings and leadership KPIs. Integration is the architecture of the brand's operating system. It is the intentional unification of UX, CX, Ops, Tech, Marketing, Real Estate, Supply Chain, Finance, and Training into one shared pattern.

When a brand is truly integrated, every new store inherits the system—not the interpretation of the system.

Every digital flow works the same way because it matches the operational model it was designed for.

Every store runs the same handoff sequence because the rules are clear and the physical design reinforces them.

Every loyalty reward behaves the same way because the mechanics were built for scalability, not improvisation.

Every packaging decision supports throughput, temperature, and production patterns.

Every part of the engine reinforces every other part. This is how integrated brands scale with confidence. They move from "Founder's Energy" to "System Energy."

The Economic Engine: Trust and Frequency

Integration becomes a compounding advantage because consistency creates trust. Trust creates habit. Habit creates frequency. And frequency is the economic engine.

Look at the emerging brands that scaled cleanly in the last decade—the ones like Wingstop, Sweetgreen, or CAVA. They didn't explode onto the national scene by accident. They grew methodically, intentionally, structurally. They created systems that could be replicated with almost eerie fidelity.

Their digital ordering experience matched the cadence of their kitchen. Their packaging held its structural integrity in busy markets and quiet markets. Their pickup areas functioned identically in suburban centers, downtown footprints, and edge-of-town outposts. Leadership could walk into a new store and know exactly what they would find. Guests could walk into any store and feel the brand without needing signage to tell them.

These brands scaled because the system did the heavy lifting. Not the individual leaders. Not the charisma of early operators. Not the brute force energy of founders. Systems scale. People strain.

Innovation Without Erosion

Perhaps the greatest advantage of integration is resilience. Integrated brands can innovate without destabilizing themselves.

A fragmented brand tries to launch a Limited Time Offer (LTO) and the wheels come off. Supply chain misses the delivery window, Ops doesn't have the training time, and Digital puts the wrong image on the app. It creates chaos.

An integrated brand launches the same LTO differently. Supply Chain aligns with Marketing on the exact window. Operations validates the build time on the KDS before the media buy is placed. Digital updates the modifier logic to ensure the kitchen isn't overwhelmed. They can deploy a menu architecture update without training chaos. They can roll out a digital redesign without collapsing operational timing.

Integration acts as a shock absorber. It allows evolution without erosion.

Fragmented brands cannot do this. Every innovation feels like an earthquake because every part of the system shakes independently. Every rollout becomes a negotiation. Every update gets compromised by store-by-store interpretation. Every improvement hits the wall of inconsistency.

Integration turns the brand into a set of working truths instead of a set of competing interpretations. This is where scale becomes possible. Real scale. Repeatable scale. Durable scale. Scale that does not dilute or drift. Scale that strengthens the identity instead of weakening it.

The brands that will define the next decade are not the ones with the loudest campaigns or the flashiest digital toys. They are the ones with the cleanest systems. Systems where digital and physical align. Systems where operational truth guides design. Systems where data informs behavior. Systems where every store delivers the same promise without effort.

Clarity compounds. Alignment accelerates. Integration scales.

And the brands that embrace integration as a discipline, not an aspiration, will own the future of this industry.

Key Takeaways: What Leaders Must Know Now

1. Departmental comfort is the real silent killer.

The old "office park" model of marketing, tech, ops, finance, and design as separate camps is not just outdated. It is hostile to how guests behave today. As long as departments defend turf, the experience will fracture.

2. Guests feel every seam you pretend does not exist.

Internal walls always become external flaws. Handoffs, misaligned priorities, and conflicting agendas show up as confusion, delays, and inconsistency in the guest journey. They do not care how you are structured. They only feel whether the chain holds.

3. Integrated organizations behave like one organism, not a committee.

The best brands treat every function as part of a single system: one circulatory system, one nervous system, one brain. Marketing, digital, ops, finance, supply chain, and training operate from shared truths, not parallel realities.

4. Integration is mechanics, not vibes.

This is not about "being more collaborative." It is about rewiring how work gets planned, launched, and measured: joint planning, shared dashboards, co-owned launches, and cross-functional reviews that make alignment unavoidable.

5. The hardest leadership move is killing departmental autonomy.

Not eliminating departments, but eliminating their ability to behave like fortified kingdoms. Integrated leaders un-encamp teams and replace, "What does my department need?" with, "What does the guest experience require, and how do we build that together?"

6. Rhythms are what keep integration from drifting.

Quarterly integrated planning, weekly or biweekly experience reviews, and cross-functional launch rituals are the scaffolding. Without them, organizations slide right back into silos and improvisation.

7. Due' Cucina is a blueprint: fix the system, not the humans.

Filippo and Davide didn't ask cooks to "try harder" or memorize more rules. They used data to build an app that absorbed complexity and gave the kitchen one clean source of truth. That is integration in practice: system intelligence replacing heroics.

8. Integrated KPIs measure system health, not local wins.

Traditional metrics celebrate department victories that often create damage elsewhere. Integrated KPIs focus on ordering-flow efficiency, digital conversion, pickup consistency, quote accuracy, reliability, accuracy, frequency, and friction — all things no single team can move alone.

9. Experience KPIs and cross-functional OKRs are the enforcement layer.

Clarity, flow, friction, and trust become the four lenses for performance. Shared OKRs like "reduce abandonment by 12 percent" or "decrease pickup variability by 20 percent" force everyone to work on the same problem, from different angles.

10. Mature brands stop measuring effort and start measuring reality.

Counting posts, campaigns, features, trainings, and meetings is motion. Measuring clarity, flow, friction, and trust is movement. Guests only feel the latter.

11. Scaling exposes truth, not potential.

Going from 5 to 500 is not about concept strength. It is about system strength. Fragmented brands scale inconsistency. Integrated brands scale reliability. One multiplies chaos. The other multiplies trust.

12. Integration becomes a compounding advantage.

Consistency → trust. Trust → habit. Habit → frequency. Frequency → economics. Integrated brands create working truths that every store inherits. That is how they grow without diluting themselves.

Action Items: What Leaders Must Do Now

1. Declare the end of department-first thinking.

Stop treating integration as a soft value.

Action:

Explicitly state in leadership forums and internal docs: "Guest experience is the first customer of every decision. Departments are support beams, not owners of the guest."

2. Stand up an Integrated Experience Council.

Not a "task force." A permanent function.

Members: Marketing, Digital/Product, Ops, Finance, IT, Supply Chain, Training, sometimes Real Estate.

Mandate:

- Own the end-to-end guest journey.
- Own the Experience KPIs and cross-functional OKRs.
- Resolve system-level tradeoffs.

3. Replace departmental quarterly plans with integrated quarterly planning.

No more marketing plan, tech plan, ops plan drafted in isolation.

Action:

- Run one quarterly planning session anchored on a single question: "What 3–5 experience improvements matter most this quarter?"
- Assign each initiative a cross-functional owner group, not a department owner.

4. Install weekly or biweekly Experience Reviews.

Make the system, not the silo, the star of the meeting.

Agenda:

Review shared KPIs: conversion, quote accuracy, pickup variability, ticket-time spread, accuracy rates, repeat behavior, loyalty friction.

Identify friction patterns and assign cross-functional fixes.

Rule: No departmental dashboards presented alone.

5. Redesign launches as co-owned events.

Campaigns, features, menu changes, and operational shifts must be jointly validated.

Checklist before launch:

Marketing: Is the promise clear and honest?

Digital: Can the flow support the promise?

Ops: Can the kitchen and FOH deliver it at peak?

Training: Do stores know how to execute?

Nothing ships until everyone signs off on feasibility.

6. Codify Experience KPIs and make them visible everywhere.

Move from "department metrics" to "experience metrics."

Action:

- Choose 1–2 metrics under each domain:
- Clarity (CTA clarity, menu legibility, wayfinding ease)
- Flow (completion rates, checkout time, throughput consistency)
- Friction (abandonment hotspots, repeated complaints, error-prone steps)
- Trust (repeat rate, reliability, accuracy, "would you return" indicators)
- Put them on a shared dashboard visible to executives and field leaders.

7. Swap activity trophies for outcome trophies.

Kill the habit of celebrating noise.

Action:

- Stop praising "X campaigns launched" or "Y features shipped."
- Start praising "reduced abandonment by 8%," "cut pickup variability by 15%," "improved accuracy by 3 points."
- Tie recognition, bonuses, and promotions to system outcomes, not departmental output.

8. Turn the Due' Cucina story into an internal case study.

Use it to rewire how the company thinks about complexity.

Action:

- Document the lesson: they used data and tech to absorb complexity, not to dump more rules on people.
- Ask of every problem: "Are we asking people to compensate, or are we fixing the system?"

9. Align your OKRs around shared behavioral outcomes.

No more "marketing OKRs" that ignore ops or "ops OKRs" that ignore digital.

Examples to deploy:

Reduce digital abandonment by X%.

Decrease pickup-time variability by Y%.

Increase first-time digital guest repeat by Z%.

Improve order accuracy by N points across all channels.

Assign: Each OKR must have at least three departments responsible.

10. Audit your reporting for effort metrics and cut them.

Go through dashboards and KPI decks.

Action:

- Tag every metric as either Activity (posts, emails, trainings, releases) or Experience (behavior, friction, performance).
- Ruthlessly deprioritize Activity metrics in executive discussions.
- If it does not change guest reality, it is secondary.

11. Systematize what already works before you scale it.

Before opening more stores or adding more channels:

Action:

- Document the current best version of: digital flow, kitchen choreography, pickup sequence, loyalty behavior, packaging, and comms.
- Turn that into a playbook with non-negotiables and flex zones.
- Every new store should inherit the system, not improvise one.

12. Make "integration or no" the filter for big decisions.

When considering any major initiative, whether it's new tech, new menu platform, new loyalty system, or a new channel, you need to ask:

Does this make integration easier or harder?

Does this unify data or fragment it?

Does this align digital and physical or drive them apart?

If the answer is "harder / fragment / apart," it is either the wrong solution or the wrong time.

EPILOGUE

The Future Belongs to Clarity

The restaurant world has never been noisier. It has never been more demanding. There are more channels to manage. There are more devices to optimize. There are more expectations to meet. There is more data than any single human can track in real time. The pressure on leaders is relentless.

The era that rewarded charisma, gut instinct, and clever campaigns has shifted. That era belonged to a linear world where you could buy attention and funnel it toward a transaction. That world is gone.

The industry now rewards brands that understand human behavior and build systems that support it with precision. Guests do not want spectacle. They want clarity. They want their time back. They want confidence in the outcome. They want to know that if they give you ten dollars and twenty minutes, you will not waste either.

The future does not belong to the loudest brand. It does not belong to the most dramatic redesign. It belongs to the organizations that operate with clarity at every layer. Clarity of promise. Clarity of flow. Clarity of system. Clarity of execution.

The future belongs to brands that respect the guest's intention, attention, and habit loops without attempting to manipulate them. It belongs to teams that treat the entire experience as one discipline rather than a collection of departmental agendas.

Clarity Is Discipline

Clarity is not poetry. Clarity is discipline. It is the work beneath the work. It is the rigor required to turn a brand from a message into a machine that performs under pressure.

Clarity is not a design aesthetic. It is an operational mandate. It emerges when teams stop trying to impress each other and begin working to remove effort from the guest's life. It appears when organizations accept that the guest owns the journey and the brand simply earns the right to participate in it. It strengthens when companies stop chasing creativity that disrupts the system and start building systems that make creativity useful.

Everything in this book leads toward the same conclusion. Clarity forms when the organization understands how the journey actually works. When it discards the Outdated Funnel and embraces the Loop. When it recognizes and dismantles its Bias Loops. When leadership aligns around systems thinking instead of personality-driven decisions. When data becomes a foundation for truth rather than an accessory for validation. When behavior shapes design. When technology becomes adaptable instead of rigid. When operational truth directs the experience instead of correcting it.

The Economic Reality of Clarity

Clarity is not just a moral good; it is a competitive weapon.

Clarity makes a brand scalable because it reduces variation. When the system is clear, it can be replicated from store number five to store number five hundred without diluting the soul of the concept.

Clarity makes a brand trustworthy because it reduces uncertainty. In a nonlinear world full of infinite choices, the brain gravitates toward the option that requires the least amount of cognitive load. Predictability is the new currency of loyalty.

Clarity makes a brand competitive because it reduces friction. Every second of hesitation removed from the ordering flow is revenue. Every moment of confusion removed from the pickup shelf is retention. Every misalignment removed from the internal team is velocity.

The brands that win the next decade will not be the ones shouting the loudest. They will be the ones removing every barrier between the guest and the value they came for. They will be the ones whose teams are so aligned internally that the seams vanish externally. They will be the ones who treat digital as the front door, operations as the brand's lived truth, and technology as the connective tissue binding everything together.

Creativity vs. Clarity

A common fear among leaders is that clarity kills the magic. They worry that systems destroy soul. This is false.

Clarity does not limit creativity. It directs it. It ensures that ideas support behavior instead of competing with it. It ensures that creativity strengthens the system rather than destabilizing it. Creativity without clarity cannot scale; it becomes noise. Creativity shaped by clarity becomes distinct, durable, and emotionally sticky because it fits the flow the guest already trusts.

When the foundation is solid, the brand can dance. When the foundation is fractured, the brand can only stumble.

The Responsibility of Choice

Clarity is chosen. It is built. It is maintained. It is protected.

That is the responsibility this book returns to you, the reader. You have the responsibility to choose clarity over convenience. You must choose clarity over ego. You must choose clarity over shortcuts. You must choose clarity over departmental borders. You must choose clarity over internal theatrics.

You have the responsibility to build systems that respect the way humans actually behave, not the way you wish they would behave. You have the responsibility to lead with a unified perspective rather than a fractured one. You have the responsibility to scale without drifting into chaos.

Clarity is not a tactic. It is an ethos. It is how brands navigate complexity without being consumed by it. It is how organizations protect their teams, strengthen their systems, and cultivate loyalty that emerges from trust rather than persuasion.

The world will only grow more chaotic. Choices will multiply. Technology will accelerate. Behavior will evolve faster than most brands can plan for. But clarity remains steady. Clarity cuts through noise. Clarity anchors decisions. Clarity compounds.

The Final Pivot

The future does not reward brands that try to impress guests. It rewards brands that work for them.

Leaders reading this face a choice. You can repeat the patterns of the past. You can hope the next campaign, the next dashboard, the next platform, or the next tactic fills the gaps. You can rely on instinct and hustle until the scale of the operation breaks the spirit of the team.

Or you can embrace the path outlined here. A path built on behavioral truth. Operational humility. Technological fluency. Cross-functional discipline.

The future does not demand perfection. It demands coherence.

The brands that choose this path will build systems that work. They will build experiences that resonate. They will build operations that scale. They will build guest relationships rooted in the unshakeable ground of trust.

They will build quieter brands. Not silent. Confident. Not flashy. Unmistakable. Not loud. Clear.

And clarity, above everything else, is what the future rewards.

FIELD GUIDE

Tools for Leaders Who Refuse to Drift

Clarity grows when leaders move from awareness to practice. The ideas in this book expose the patterns that quietly undermine restaurant brands, and the tools in this section give you a way to confront those patterns with structure and intention. These are working tools, built to sit inside real meetings, guide real decisions, and support teams that want stronger alignment and steadier execution.

Leaders often reach a moment while reading when the problems on the page match the problems in their organization. The symptoms feel familiar. The decisions feel familiar. The drift feels familiar. When that recognition hits, the next step needs to be simple and direct.

This Field Guide gives you the practical scaffolding to start. Use these tools with your team. Print them. Argue over them. Redo them. Tape them to the wall of your office. They are designed to create forward motion, to turn clarity into behavior, and to help you rebuild your brand with intention rather than inertia.

What follows is a set of simple, powerful frameworks:

A diagnostic to identify which Quiet Killer is undermining your brand

A visual model to anchor your operating system

A weekly ritual that keeps you from drifting

A 90 day plan to build real, measurable momentum

Each tool creates a different form of clarity. The diagnostic reveals the forces shaping your current behavior. The operating system diagram organizes your work into a clear sequence. The weekly audit establishes a new rhythm for leadership conversations. The 90 day plan turns intention into movement with a timeline anyone can follow.

You do not need to master everything at once. You only need to begin. Clarity grows with movement, not perfection.

Let's get to work.

Quiet Killers Diagnostic

A 10-Minute Assessment for Leadership Teams

This diagnostic helps you identify which of the Quiet Killers is most active inside your organization. Use it to surface the patterns your team has normalized and to set a clear starting point for change. The goal is simple: see the reality you're working with before choosing your next move.

Read each statement and score your agreement from 1 to 5.

1 = Strongly disagree

5 = Strongly agree

Killer One: The Funnel Fantasy

Our marketing decisions assume a linear, predictable customer journey.

We rely on broad, top-down campaigns more than behavior-based insights.

We measure success with metrics that ignore how guests actually decide.

Subtotal Killer One: _____

Killer Two: The Bias Loop

We often adopt ideas because other brands use them first.

We chase "best in class" tools instead of what fits our operational reality.

We regularly confuse popular success stories with strategic truth.

Subtotal Killer Two: _____

Killer Three: The Convenience Trap

We choose solutions that are easy to implement rather than right for the guest.

We reduce problems to marketing issues when they're actually operational.

We prioritize short-term wins over long-term coherence.

Subtotal Killer Three: _____

Killer Four: Identity Drift

Our brand's internal behavior contradicts the story we tell externally.

Our teams cannot articulate the belief our brand is built on.

We change direction frequently, depending on who's in the room.

Subtotal Killer Four: _____

Interpretation

Highest score: Your dominant Quiet Killer. This is where your transformation begins.

Second highest: Your drag force. This is where behaviors will resist progress.

Lowest scores: These will become vulnerabilities if ignored during change.

If two killers tie, choose the one that feels most urgent or most visible to the guest experience.

The Clarity Operating System Map

The Clarity Operating System organizes the work of building a coherent brand into a clear and repeatable structure. It anchors the model introduced in Part III and brings the full process into a single view. Use it as a reference point for planning, alignment, and decision making as you reshape your brand's behavior and experience.

THE CLARITY OPERATING SYSTEM

1. Detect

Identify which Quiet Killers are active. Assess current behaviors, gaps, friction points, and decision patterns.

Goal: Replace assumption with awareness.

2. Align

Unify leaders, teams, and partners around a clear belief, shared priorities, and expected behaviors.

Goal: Everyone rows in the same direction.

3. Design

Shape the brand's messaging, experience, and operating behaviors to reinforce belief.

Goal: Build coherence between what the brand says and what the brand does.

4. Deliver

Execute consistently across channels, teams, and touchpoints.

Goal: Turn clarity into practice the guest can feel.

5. Reinforce

Measure, refine, and strengthen. Identify drift early. Adjust without abandoning the belief.

Goal: Turn brand clarity into a compounding advantage.

Monday Morning Audit

A 15-Minute Weekly Ritual to Prevent Drift

Clarity weakens when teams move through the week without reflection or alignment. The Monday Morning Audit creates a steady rhythm for leadership conversations and keeps attention on the choices that matter. This brief ritual reveals drift early, reinforces expected behaviors, and grounds each week in intention rather than reaction.

Ask and answer these five questions honestly:

1. What strengthened clarity last week?

Identify the actions, decisions, or conversations that reinforced belief or improved coherence.

2. What weakened clarity last week?

Call out the shortcuts, compromises, or misaligned decisions that slipped through.

3. Where did a Quiet Killer show up?

Did you fall into survivorship thinking? A convenience decision? Identity drift? A funnel fantasy?

4. What decision this week requires clarity over convenience?

Name it before you face it. You cannot fight a killer you won't name.

5. Who needs alignment this week?

Clarity breaks first where communication is weakest. Identify the person or group who needs reinforcement.

Instructions for Use

Keep it short.

Keep it real.

Review answers monthly to spot patterns.

Share takeaways with your team for accountability.

The 90-Day Clarity Plan

Leaders often need a clear path once they recognize the work ahead. The First 90 Days Plan offers a structured sequence for building momentum and installing new habits across the organization. Each 30 day phase focuses on a different part of the operating system so teams can move with direction, pace, and shared understanding.

THE FIRST 90 DAYS OF KILLING YOUR QUIET KILLERS

Days 1–30: Detect + Align

Objective: Build awareness and unify the leadership core.

Actions:

Run the Quiet Killers Diagnostic with the full leadership team.

Identify your dominant and secondary killers.

Map the top friction points in guest experience and internal communication.

Facilitate a 60-minute Alignment Session to articulate the brand's belief and operational priorities.

Identify 1–2 high-urgency issues where clarity must replace convenience immediately.

Deliverables:

Diagnostic results summary

Team alignment statement

Priority list for first 90 days

Days 31–60: Design

Objective: Rebuild communication, behavior, and experience to reinforce belief.

Actions:

Audit all messaging for clarity and coherence.

Audit guest journey friction.

Audit operational contradictions (e.g., marketing promises vs store reality).

Rebuild the core messaging layer around belief.

Choose three Proof Behaviors that demonstrate belief in action.

Create a simple design plan for how belief shows up in the guest experience.

Deliverables:

Updated core messaging

List of Proof Behaviors

A belief-driven experience map

A shortlist of 2–3 quick wins to build momentum

Days 61–90: Deliver + Reinforce

Objective: Execute consistently and establish new leadership habits.

Actions:

Launch the first Proof Behavior (guest-facing or internal).

Install the Monday Morning Audit.

Build the Brand Behavior Scorecard and begin tracking monthly.

Hold a drift review session: identify early slippage and close gaps.

Revisit the dominant Quiet Killer to assess improvement.

Deliverables:

First Proof Behavior activated

Weekly Monday Morning Audit rituals installed

Monthly Behavior Scorecard baseline

End-of-quarter clarity report

Updated Quiet Killers Diagnostic to measure movement

Outcome of the 90-Day Plan

By the end of 90 days, leaders will have:

A shared belief

A unified operating model

A clear behavioral roadmap

A brand increasingly free of Quiet Killers

A team that has tasted the advantage of clarity

Momentum becomes the new normal.

Bibliography

Core Behavioral & Decision Science

Kahneman, Daniel. Thinking, Fast and Slow. Farrar, Straus and Giroux, 2011.

Damasio, Antonio. Descartes' Error: Emotion, Reason, and the Human Brain. G.P. Putnam's Sons, 1994.

University College London. Research on cognitive load, task abandonment, and decision friction in high-intent environments.

Marketing Theory, Funnels & Behavioral Models

Lewis, E. St. Elmo. AIDA Model. Circa 1898. Foundational advertising framework later distorted into modern funnel thinking.

Google. Decoding Decisions: The Messy Middle. Think with Google, 2020.

Boston Consulting Group. Move Beyond the Linear Funnel. BCG Research.

Sharp, Byron. How Brands Grow. Oxford University Press.

Irwin, Todd. De-Positioning: The Secret Brand Strategy for Creative Competitive Advantage. Wiley.

Digital Experience, UX & Conversion Research

Baymard Institute. Research on checkout usability, forced account creation, and conversion abandonment.

Google. Mobile Page Speed Benchmarks and conversion impact research.

Gartner. Digital Commerce Platforms research and replatforming studies.

Operations, Systems & Organizational Design

McKinsey & Company. Research on operational complexity, organizational drag, and incremental decision bias.

Bain & Company. Studies on productivity loss from fragmented systems and operational inefficiency.

Restaurant Industry Case Studies & Reporting

The Wall Street Journal. Coverage of Chipotle's operational reset and post-crisis recovery.

CNBC. Reporting on McDonald's digital infrastructure, kiosk rollout, and internal replatforming challenges.

Chipotle Mexican Grill, Inc. Public earnings reports and investor communications (2016–2022).

Technology, Pricing & Public Response

Wendy's Company. Earnings call transcripts and public statements related to dynamic pricing and digital menu boards (2023–2024).

U.S. media coverage and public response to Wendy's dynamic pricing announcement, 2024.

Original Frameworks & Prior Works

Szala, Joseph. The Bullhearted Brand. Bullhearted Creative Co.

Szala, Joseph. Mass Behaving. Bullhearted Creative Co.

Szala, Joseph. Quiet Killers Diagnostic, Brand Behavior Scorecard, and Alignment Frameworks. Original work.

Index

A

ability	34
accuracy	113, 121, 125-126
action	7, 15-16, 85
advantage	65
agency	70
alignment	55, 66, 78-80, 82-85, 123
analysis	97
analytics	100, 102, 104
anchor	94
anchored	30
approach	54, 121
approached	122
attention	7
awareness	10, 52-53

B

Barrel	26
behave	52-53
behaved	10
behavior	9, 11-13, 17, 36, 53, 57, 60, 72-74, 84, 88, 94, 98, 100, 102-103, 107, 109, 111, 119, 125, 132
behavioral	55, 65, 89, 91-92, 98, 100, 109-110, 121, 124
belief	101
believed	7
believes	83
belongs	71, 131-132
between	14, 18, 104, 119
bigger	66
biggest	73
brands	2, 4, 10-11, 16, 19, 23-24, 29-31, 33, 35-36, 38, 41, 53, 65-67, 69, 77, 82-83, 85, 89-91, 97-99, 103, 105, 107, 109, 112-114, 116-117, 119, 123-124, 128-129, 132-133
breaks	65
broken	29, 103
building	54, 70, 120
builds	42, 69, 119
business	83

C

campaign	71, 87, 103, 121
campaigns	45, 101
category	52, 61-62

century	11
Chipotle	37-39
choice	52-53, 94
choices	52, 90
choose	36, 60, 117, 133
chooses	39
clarity	4, 11, 14, 18-20, 27, 33, 37, 39, 54-55, 57, 63-75, 78-79, 82, 88-89, 92-94, 109, 117, 131-133
cognitive	13, 18, 56, 105
coherence	94
collapsed	48
collective	85
collide	13
commerce	36
companies	35
company	44, 84
competitor	99
complaints	73
complete	12
complexity	1
conceptual	26
conditions	122
confidence	15
conform	36
Consistent	93
consumers	60
content	16
continuous	119
control	16, 117
convenient	3
conversion	10, 124
corporate	48
correctly	63
counter	113
counts	101
create	3, 13, 30, 33, 92
created	11, 41, 43
creates	3, 57, 72, 79, 128
creation	12
creative	26, 69-71
creativity	69, 71, 132
crisis	37
Cucina	122
curbside	106
customer	73
customers	7

D

dashboards	17
decision	27-28, 38, 62-63, 65, 96
decisions	9, 13-14, 23-24, 27, 42-43, 60-62, 67, 69, 72, 80, 82, 93, 119
dedication	66
deeper	10
deliver	112
delivery	38, 62
delusion	98
demand	42
demands	16, 26, 69, 119
department	67, 80-81
deserves	11
design	4, 11, 13, 16, 28, 57, 82-84, 88, 91, 114
designed	7, 10, 92
designing	20, 104
desire	7
determine	92
dictates	117
difference	24
different	3, 23, 77, 102, 119
difficult	3

digital 11-12, 16-17, 19-20, 23, 29-30, 34, 36, 38, 42-48, 53-57, 70, 74, 77, 80-81, 84-85, 88, 91, 93, 98, 103-104, 106, 108-109, 112-117, 120-121, 123, 125-126, 128-129
digitally 109
direction 25-26, 69
directly 101
directs 132
discipline 37, 83, 127, 132
diverge 44
driven 96
drive-thru 18
drop-off 100
during 59

E

economics 72
effort 94, 101, 105, 127
egress 54
emotional 25, 60, 93
encounter 44
energy 93
engaged 78
engagement 17
engine 16, 91, 128
enterprise 23-24
estate 83-84
evaluate 81
evaluates 59
evaluation 59, 89-90
evolution 26
evolve 99
execution 119
experience 3-4, 18, 20, 32, 48, 62, 66, 68, 70, 77-78, 80-81, 83-85, 87-92, 94, 99, 115, 119-121, 123-125, 132

F

failures 24
faster 33, 46, 57
fastest 62
feature 25
features 24, 110, 117
Filippo 122
Finance 47, 67-68, 77, 84
fluidly 78
footprint 24
forced 10, 12, 116
forces 19, 88, 92, 99, 101, 119, 121
foundation 95
founders 122
fragmented 48, 127
frameworks 41
frequency 93-94, 125, 128
friction 13, 18, 25, 54, 80, 91, 93, 99-101, 104-105, 114-117, 121, 124
functional 12, 44
funnel 6-7, 9-20, 54-55, 98
funnels 12-13
future 131, 133

G

gimmick 116
Google 9, 13-14, 52, 60, 90, 109-111
growth 41
guests 2-4, 10, 12-14, 16-17, 26-27, 30, 38, 48, 52-57, 60-62, 88-89, 94, 98-101, 103-104, 106, 108-111, 124-125
guidance 93

H

habitual 62
handle 77

handoff	113	**K**	
hardware	81	killer	2
heartbeat	114	killers	2, 4, 30, 49
hesitation	93	kitchen	32, 112, 116, 122
heuristics	60	Korean	59

I

identity	66, 111	**L**	
ignored	30	language	65
impact	105, 121	latest	71
impulses	7	launch	121
increase	80, 90	layers	91-92
increases	110	leaders	2-3, 29, 32, 43, 62, 97
Indecision	107	leadership	3, 25, 29, 43, 48, 70
industry	37, 43	leading	70
influence	57, 66, 90	lifeblood	69
influenced	43	lifestyle	70
inside	17, 97	limitation	115
instincts	97	linear	10, 14, 55
Integrated	3, 119, 121, 123-124, 126-128	locations	81
intent	56-57	longer	68, 81, 122
intention	13, 19	long-term	36, 82
interest	7	loyalty	3, 10-12, 17, 19, 24, 42, 45, 47, 74, 80, 94, 98, 100, 107, 111, 115, 125, 128
interface	69		
internal	34		
internally	78	luxury	7, 73
introduces	18		
invested	116	**M**	
invisible	30, 99-100	majority	62
invitation	11	market	83-85
		marketers	7
J		marketing	3, 10, 32, 37, 41-48, 54, 65, 67-69, 77-80, 83-85, 101, 103, 109, 119-121, 123, 126, 128
Jaguar	71, 73		
journey	12, 14, 16-19, 55, 57, 78, 89, 107, 132	markets	129
		MarTech	102
		McDonald	23

meaning	73	obvious	110
measure	123-124, 127	offering	62
measured	41, 79	operate	4
mechanics	24	operating	104

operations 32, 37, 41-48, 67-68, 77, 79-80, 83-85, 100-101, 103, 113-114, 116, 119-121, 123, 126

memory	34, 94		
Mendocino	78		
mental	93	opposite	27
metrics	80, 85, 101	OpsTech	102-103
Middle	14, 16, 52, 57, 60-61	optimize	13, 63
mindset	82	optimizes	47
misaligned	13	optimizing	34
mission	41	option	19
mobile	13, 113, 116	options	37, 55

ordering 3, 11, 19-20, 34, 54, 74, 81, 115-116

modern	11, 15, 57		
modifiers	115	orders	106

moment 2, 11, 13, 16, 19-20, 45, 52, 56-57, 59, 90, 101, 109

		ordinary	71
		outdated	4
moments	11, 57, 84	outperform	110
momentum	85	ownership	83
movement	19		
Mugatu	71		
muscle	34	**P**	
mystery	13	paired	46
		pattern	27, 33, 53, 93
		patterns	17, 102, 110-111, 125

people 2, 7, 9, 14-16, 23, 29, 48, 60, 70, 73, 89, 97

N

national	128	percent	126
nearly	34	persuasion	2, 7, 12-14, 20, 52, 56, 60
needed	9, 11, 41	phenomenon	52
negative	125	physical	45, 60, 84, 91, 112-113
nonlinear	78, 120		

pickup 18, 34, 46-47, 60, 80, 88, 93, 100, 112-113, 124

nostalgia	26		
number	110	picture	80
numbers	71, 97, 103, 124	planning	83, 121
		platform	34, 36, 105, 117

O

platforms	32, 35-36, 104, 117	rebrand	26
points	54	rebuilt	37
precision	2, 122	redemption	114, 125
predictive	107	reduce	80, 90, 105
pressure	32, 98, 122	reduces	72, 132
priorities	41, 121	reducing	101, 110
prioritize	106	reflect	13, 116
problem	43, 46, 48, 66, 77	reflects	74
problems	32, 41	reinforces	74, 128
process	57, 94	relaxes	65
processes	3	release	71
product	66, 70	removes	68, 93
profile	106	report	125
promise	36, 45, 59, 71, 92, 112, 123	required	38
promises	112	research	97, 124
promotion	46	resistance	101
promotions	46, 73	responsive	32
prototype	84-85	restart	15
proximity	60	restaurant	6-7, 9-11, 13-14, 16, 18-20, 22-23, 28-29, 32-33, 36-38, 41-42, 44, 52-53, 56-57, 62-63, 65, 69, 72, 74, 77, 80-83, 89, 92, 97, 99, 102-103, 108-109, 112, 115, 119-120, 124-125
purchase	52		
purpose	2, 59, 66		
		return	94, 100
Q		revealed	110
quality	43, 66	reveals	98, 102
quarter	83	reviews	60, 121
quarterly	121	reward	123, 128
question	16, 121	rewards	133
questions	104	Rework	32
quietly	9	ritual	85
		rituals	121
R			
Raising	74	**S**	
realities	30, 84	safety	37
reality	2, 7, 14, 23-24, 80, 85, 112	sandwich	74
reason	25		

Scaling	127
screen	71, 100
sentiment	125
sequence	7, 81, 89
service	106
shared	19, 78-80, 85, 121
shifts	98
shortcut	115-116
shortcuts	33-35, 56, 60, 69, 71-72, 115, 117
shouting	89
signals	125
silent	100
similar	30
simple	110
simply	10
single	80
slightly	72
smaller	23
social	52
solving	33
spikes	92
started	73
starts	17
station	112
stores	34
strain	32
strategy	2, 55, 74
stress	43
structural	32, 115
structure	29, 43
structures	41, 48
struggled	116
succeeded	24
success	3, 24, 41, 79
successes	23
supports	59
surface	2, 106
survival	33
swears	41
Sweetgreen	74
switch	14, 56
switching	36
system	4, 10, 14, 18, 29, 32, 34, 36, 38, 43, 76, 78, 88-89, 94, 99, 101, 105-107, 113, 115-117, 119-124, 126-129, 132
systems	3-4, 33-36, 38, 41-42, 45, 81, 92, 107, 112, 114-117, 123-124, 128-129, 132-133

T

tactic	133
tasked	42
tech-first	82
technology	3-4, 23, 35-36, 41-42, 69, 77, 81, 83-85, 119, 123, 132
templates	115
temporary	34
tension	18
thinking	11, 14, 16
thinks	103
thrive	4
throughput	112
timing	98
together	78, 94, 120-121, 123
transform	79
treated	30
treats	12, 57
triggered	43
triggers	53, 59

U

unclear	111
understand	57, 91, 103

undone	61
unified	80, 84, 103-104
universal	53
update	129
updated	46
uptime	41
urgency	33

V

validation	97
valuable	69
variations	122
vehicle	71, 73
vehicles	73
vendor	38, 115
Vendors	36
version	45
visible	23
volume	114, 122

W

waiting	114
wandering	107
wanted	30, 56, 70
website	2, 53
websites	109
winners	24
workflow	43
working	42

Y

yellow	28
younger	60

About the Author

Joseph is a brand strategy and identity designer based in North Carolina. His skills go far deeper than that though. He currently serves as Vice President and Partner at 3Owl, a digital transformation powerhouse focused on designing and building joyously revolutionary experiences.

Prior to joining 3Owl, Joseph founded and built a restaurant branding agency that actively led the branding, rebranding, and marketing charge for over 200 restaurant brands. As a thought leader, Joseph has written articles published by leading publications like QSR Magazine, Nation's Restaurant News, Bloomberg, Business Insider, Branders Magazine, and Vox. He has served as sources for journalists on trending topics in the restaurant and branding industries and written multiple books on restaurant branding and marketing.

He is the founder and former host of Forktales, a restaurant-focused podcast, and the founder of Grits & Grids, the number one restaurant branding media channel. His bullhearted nature keeps him at the forefront of trends and shifts in the restaurant digital revolution. He still loves McDonald's, and isn't afraid to say it.

www.ingramcontent.com/pod-product-compliance
Lightning Source LLC
LaVergne TN
LVHW072337080526
838199LV00122B/605/J